Myth, Magic, and Marketing

An Irreverent History of Branding
From The Acropolis to The Apple Store:

By Walt Kuenstler

Contents

Zolexa Publishing

614 Darby Road

Havertown, PA 19083

www.zolexaltd.com

Dedication

This book is dedicated to my father, Walter Pershing Kuenstler, who introduced me to marketing, advertising, and branding (not to mention Tang™).

Acknowledgements

Dr. Katherine Morris led me to the worlds of mythology and Jungian psychology. Thanks to her wisdom, I realized that the ancient gods and the Brand Gods function similarly.

Joseph McIntyre and Robert Kiss were my first marketing mentors, at the Sieber & McIntyre agency in Chicago, where I began my professional odyssey as an 18-year-old office boy in 1967.

Victoria Ipri has been my editor, bringing shape, cohesion, and clarity to this manuscript. She is a master wordsmith, and a brilliant marketer in her own right.

The Starbucks in Bala Cynwyd, Pennsylvania provided a clean well-lit place where this book came into being over hundreds of doppio espressos and tall iced teas. Special thanks go to baristas Dwayne and BJ who always had a smile.

Introduction—
The Myth and Magic of the Brand Gods

After all, people don't buy things to have things. They buy things to work for them. They buy hope—hope of what your merchandise will do for them.

—Helen Landon Cass,
speaking to retail executives in 1926

Branding is as old as mankind.

Branding made civilization possible.

Heck, maybe branding *is* civilization.

I have spent a lifetime working in the world of advertising, marketing, and branding. To the man with a hammer, everything looks like a nail. To the guy who creates advertising for a living, the entire universe can be contained in a 30 second TV spot.

Our monkey ancestors began creating the elements essential for branding the moment they started to develop language, symbolism, abstract thinking, and the concept of the supernatural.

They were also picking fleas off each other, in an example of an *unmet consumer need* that was not to be satisfied until several millennia later, with the advent of Sargeant's Flea Collar.

Then, as now, the quest for solutions to life's problems (including persistent itching) was intrinsic to the human condition. This is why I suggest that branding was essential to the creation of civilization. After all, language, symbolism, abstract thinking, and a sense of the magical are essential to both civilization and modern branding.

Which, of course, brings us to erectile dysfunction (Ok, I admit the segue is limp, but allow me a Cialis moment...).

If I was an ancient Greek man having difficulty lifting my olive branch (metaphorically speaking), a cure for that humiliation was not a little blue pill, but *Priapus*, the Greek god of male fertility. Appropriately, he was the lustful son of Aphrodite and Dionysus, gods of love and wine. Even then, good breeding was important.

I'd like to show you a picture of Priapus, but this book is intended for a family audience. Suffice to say that a pair of extra baggy trousers would have to be Photoshopped onto his statue to clear the family values censors. Archaeologists seldom doubted whether a statue they had unearthed in Athens was Priapus ("Hey, Dr. Michelson, look at the size of THAT thing!").

Greek men in togas seeking greater virility would make offerings to Priapus before a hot date or the Acropolis High School prom.

This sort of magic was not unique to the Greeks.

A Viking having problems with his lutefisk would turn to the god Freyr.

The Egyptians relied on Min, the god of male virility, to ensure Cleopatra's needle was indeed fit for a queen. Blushing Victorian-era Egyptologists would only take waist-up photographs of Min, or otherwise find ways to cover his most significant characteristic.

The point? Way before the wizards at Pfizer brought Viagra to market, mankind found a branded solution to this problem. The many ancient and pagan gods promised to grant wishes of health, wealth, wisdom, sexuality, love. Those same promises can be found any time, day or night, just by clicking though the channels on your cable box.

Imagine the sales patter at the Temple of Priapus around 400 BC.

"Yep, never fails. Our statue of Priapus has been crafted using the finest white marble, polished to perfection by certified virgins, and painted with only the freshest ox blood, to insure the most powerful fertility icon the world has ever known."

The only thing missing was an 800 number and a tiny disclaimer, *"No promise of performance for the Priapus figurine is made or implied. Statuette is for entertainment purposes only. Choking hazard - keep away from small children. Do not microwave. In the event of an erection lasting longer than four hours, shout 'Holy Hosanna' repeatedly."*

Today, of course, you need only tune to any NFL game to learn that Priapus now has many names—Cialis, Viagra, and Levitra among them. These have become our magical new gods of virility. This is the essence of what I call the Brand Gods.

Consumers, eager to find quick, easy, magical solutions that solve their problems and satisfy their needs become willing converts to whatever product offers the most enticing brand gospel.

Tyler Wigg Stevenson, a theologian who explores the role of branding in our contemporary spiritual life, notes that society's rampant consumerism is fueled, in part, by a collective imagination that assigns magical value to material objects. In other words, we turn what we buy into god-like objects.

In our hearts, a Mercedes is not simply a car, and Nike's Air Jordan XVIIs are more than sneakers. Each embodies the mystique and status of luxury, and the promise of unequalled performance. "These transcendent, archetypal, values of luxury and performance live in the minds of the purchasers who drive our consumerist economy, and who give *consumerism* its power through their fierce devotion," says Stevenson.

While science may have replaced the supernatural in our public conversation, ancient cravings for heavenly solutions to life's problems still heat our blood. And our VISA cards.

Today those solutions appear not as ancient gods, but as brands. This, then, is the myth and magic behind modern marketing.

The Origins of Branding— or One Martini, Two Martini...

Advertising is based on one thing: happiness. And do you know what happiness is? Happiness is the smell of a new car. It's freedom from fear. It's a billboard on the side of a road that screams with reassurance that whatever you're doing is OK. You are OK.

— Don Draper in Mad Men

As a callow eighteen year old starting my first job as an office boy at Chicago's Seiber & McIntyre advertising agency in 1967, I viewed advertising, marketing, and branding as recent phenomena that flourished primarily in the decades following World War II.

I was wrong.

The roots of modern advertising and branding extend back at least two hundred years, long before the Mad Men of my era were born.

Every religion worth its salt has a creation story – a Genesis myth explaining how the world began.

Advertising, marketing, and the Brand Gods have their own Genesis story. To borrow a page from today's tea-drinking fundamentalist anti-Darwinists, our contemporary consumerist society is no accident of random evolution. No, our materialist culture is definitely the result of intelligent design.

The family tree of advertising has roots extending back to the early 1800s, when captivating pitchmen sold patent medicines all across America, promising to cure all ills of the human body and spirit. Anacin's claim of "fast, Fast, FAST RELIEF!" traces its origin to patent medicines sold in England during the American Revolution. England's royal family would grant favored merchants a license, or patent, for their medical elixirs. Crossing the Atlantic to the Colonies, such patent medicines became a widespread and profitable business by the middle of the 19th century.

The formulas for most 19th century medicines were not officially patented, as we understand that term today. Their ingredients, almost never listed on the label, were primarily alcohol, laced with vegetable extracts and herbs. As you might suspect, these potions were of questionable therapeutic value, and more than one customer died after taking a dose.

Nonetheless, people were desperately searching for cures to their ailments, and we can imagine that the immediate relief provided by a stiff dose of flavored alcohol seemed magical at the time. Those clever pitchmen created some of the original brand myths, insisting that their secret recipes came from lost African tribes, from Indian medicine men, or from the archives of ancient wizards.

These remedies claimed to cure or prevent everything from venereal diseases and tuberculosis to colic, indigestion, and even cancer. Women sought to find relief from their monthly discomforts. Paradoxically, some were sold as hangover cures.

To attract large audiences of potential purchasers, these pitchmen staged elaborate productions—part-circus, part-carnival, and part-theatre—known as *medicine shows.* Note that, since the 1950's, network television has used similar spectacles, from the *Ed Sullivan Show* to the annual outsized Super Bowl extravaganza, to attract a crowd.

One such pitchman, a clever fellow known as Nevada Ned, described those extravaganzas as a "full evening of vaudeville, musical comedy, Wild West shows, minstrels, magic, burlesque, dog and pony circuses, not to mention Punch and Judy, pantomime, movies, menagerie, bands, parades and pie eating contests." Too bad Ned didn't have an *@piecontest* Twitter feed.

Myth and magic were integral to marketing patent medicine products. Dr. C. M. Townsend sold his Magic Oil with the slogan, "Why let pain your pleasures spoil, for want of Townsend's Magic Oil?" John Austen Hamlin, a traveling magician, greatly increased his income with the introduction of Wizard Oil liniment, which promised magical healing.

The magic did not always work. Following any number of unfortunate poisonings and even deaths, the era of the patent medicine pitchman began to fade after 1906, with the passage of the federal Pure Food and Drug Law, aimed at regulating the ingredients of such potions. Thus, cocaine was removed from Coca-Cola and miraculous claims required substantiation.

The advertising industry still strives to live down its reputation for deception, clever wording, and false claims established during the patent medicine heyday. Dead customers will have that effect.

The promise of magical self-transformation through the ritual of purchase provides the basic rationale for much contemporary consumer advertising. Today's screaming infomercials, epitomized by the late Billy Mays, are living fossils, descended directly from Nevada Ned, P.T. Barnum, and a thousand other now-anonymous snake oil pitchmen.

Advertising was well established as a distinct profession by 1900, playing an essential role in lubricating the vast economic machine that transformed America from a self-sufficient agrarian society into an urbanized colossus driven by the materialistic need to consume more and more.

Business thinkers of the time described a virtuous cycle:

- Mass production created millions of new factory jobs, increasing consumers' incomes...

- Increased incomes allowed the purchase of more and more goods, produced ever more cheaply, thanks to factory mass production...

- Those purchases created income for factory owners, leading to the creation of more and more factories...

- More and more factories led to more and more jobs, generating more and more consumer spending, enabling the creation of more factories.

In his 1928 book, *American Prosperity*, investment banker and management visionary Paul Mazur, wrote that America had changed from a *needs* culture to a *desires* culture —that people were now "trained to desire change, to want new things even before the old have been entirely consumed... Man's desires can be developed so that they will greatly overshadow his needs." The hunger for massive consumption had become a virtue, propelling a surging economy to ever-greater heights.

This concept, of course, lies at the heart of materialism, and remains the Holy Grail for consumer marketers, retailers, and manufacturers.

In 1928 Mazur wrote, "A staggering machine has been built to satisfy consumer demand and even the consumer's whispered interest. The machine is here. It now has an appetite of its own which must be satisfied."

The machine *"has an appetite of its own which must be satisfied."*

Elaborating in the Harvard Business Review, Mazur wrote, "The machinery which has developed consumer demands has become so completely accepted that we forget our *duty* to it."

We have a *duty to the machine.*

"...The safety of the industrial superstructure depends upon the strengths of the marketing foundations, just as the foundation would have no value without the industrial structure."

Without those *marketing foundations,* the whole of society crumbles.

In the Introduction to this book, I assert that branding could be equated with civilization itself. My tongue was in my cheek. But on page 205 of *Fables of Abundance,* I discover that author Jackson Lears writes, "Some spokesmen for the [advertising] industry, assuming that advertising was the solution to the problem of distribution, moved from that assumption to *equate advertising with civilization itself.*"

Andre Siegfried, a French academic and political writer known for his commentaries on American society, observed in 1928, "From a *moral point of view,* it is obvious that Americans have come to consider their standard of living as a somewhat sacred acquisition, which they will defend at any price. This means that they would be ready to make many an intellectual or even moral concession in order to maintain that standard."

You may remember that in 2003 President George W. Bush urged Americans to "go shopping" as a patriotic duty to combat terrorism. Imagine Patrick Henry holding off the British with his VISA card, proclaiming, "I regret that I have but fifty thousand Reward Points to give for my country."

As the profession of advertising matured and found definition, philosophies of selling and persuasion emerged. "It is a great responsibility to mold the daily lives of millions of our fellow men, and I am persuaded that we are second only to statesmen and editors in power for good," wrote adman James Wallen in 1925. Advertising had become a noble calling.

With the support of leading businessmen of the time, Harvard University created its famed School of Business in 1908. This was the first school to offer a masters degree in business administration, the MBA.

Harvard would take the lead in teaching American business how to sell more. Among its initial offerings were courses on advertising, merchandising, and retailing. In 1914, Harvard's required course *Economic Resources of the United States* was renamed *Marketing*.

Paul Mazur's machine was being fed.

A Harvard professor named Paul Cherington authored the first textbook devoted to the subject of advertising in 1914. Cherington noted that his definition of marketing included "the whole process of physical distribution, *demand activation,* merchandising, pricing, and other activities."

I love that phrase *demand activation.* I'm considering it as the slogan for my next company.

Cherington's explanation of branding in a 1915 issue of The Rotarian magazine has stood the test of time:

"For instance, take a can of corn. If it has no label, it is simply a plain, white tin can. As a maker or of a dealer in canned corn, I can offer it to you, and no matter what I say to you about it in my personal salesmanship, you are skeptical. If, however, I put a label on it, you at once feel a certain amount of confidence that probably the can really does contain corn. And if, perchance, the label contains a claim that it is a superior grade of Honey-sweet Maine corn, the confidence is increased, and if it also bears a distinctive name, and the name of some responsible company packing or selling it, it takes on an entirely new aspect. The consumer, buying this corn, not only buys merchandise, but he buys and pays for all the claims made for it, and he also buys and pays for the possibility of securing another can just like it whenever he wants it."

At the end of World War I, The New York School of Fine And Applied Arts hired a gentleman named Frank Alvah Parsons to teach classes in display advertising and product design. Parsons urged his students to appeal to the imagination of consumers—to their psychology (this was the age of Freud). He advocated sales messages based on the *sex appeal of objects*.

"Art is not for the few, for the talented, for the genius, for the rich, nor the church," Parsons said in 1920. "Industry is the nation's life, art is the quality of beauty in expression, and industrial art is the cornerstone of our national art."

Fifty years, later and sounding a bit like Parsons, Camille Paglia wrote in *Break, Blow, Burn:* "I recognized commercial popular culture as the authentic native voice of America." Paglia, a noted American author, teacher, social critic, and dissident feminist, suggests that those who create our advertising help shape our culture, saying, "Advertising is an art form" when interviewed for the Yale Journal of Ethics in 1996.

Paglia says, "Religion, ritual, and art began as one, and a religious or metaphysical element is still present in all art..." And if advertising is art, religion and ritual resonate in its song. "Popular culture is the great heir to the western past."

Under Parsons' leadership, the New York School of Fine Art and Applied Arts was transformed into The Parsons School of Design. And, yes, students at its campus in France invented the ubiquitous Parsons table.

"The American conception of advertising is to arouse desires and stimulate wants, to make people dissatisfied with the old and out-of-date and by constant iteration to send them out to work harder to get the latest model—whether that model be an icebox or a rug or a new home," explained ad man Bruce Barton during a 1929 radio broadcast.

Pioneered at the turn of the twentieth century, the concept that what is *new* is magical, while what is *old* has lost its power and its energy, has been an essential element driving consumers to keep consuming. Even today, the iPhone is succeeded by the 3G model, which is soon trumped by the 4S edition. The new gods are stronger than the old gods.

Warren Abrams, my client at the New York Times, recalled his time as an advertising manager with Plymouth. Headlines introducing the new 1957 Plymouth models shouted, "Suddenly it's 1960!" Tomorrow is always better than today.

Amos Parrish, a fashion consultant in the 1920's, taught, "Nothing is going to stop fashion. It wears things out. And industry wants things worn out in order to make more things to build bigger businesses to pay larger dividends. Things must grow. Fashion is the one thing in the world that will do it. And without fashion it won't be done. But it will be done."

Earnest Elmo Calkins, who founded his advertising agency Calkins and Holden in 1901, waxed eloquent about the beauty of planned obsolescence. Writing in the *Journal of Political Economy*, Calkins advocated the concept of *consumer engineering,* which involved the creation of demand through advertising. He asked why any woman would want last year's fashion when this year's fashion was so much more attractive. "Does there seem to be a sad waste in this process? Not at all. Wearing things out does not produce prosperity. Buying things does."

Suddenly it's 1960!

Rational arguments were even put forth in favor of shabbily manufactured goods as a means to stimulate demand. That same article in that 1901 issue of the Journal *of Political Economy* said, "It is often claimed that lower prices often mean inferior goods, which must be replaced long before the difference in price is made up in the wear of the article. May it not be argued on the other hand that this seeming inferiority has a distinct social value? Cleanliness is increased, disease prevented, choice stimulated, variety made possible, and the standard of living raised by buying less durable goods." You can imagine a bizzaro *Consumer Reports* recommending products that fall apart faster than their competitors, because this keeps things cleaner!

Radio personality Helen Landon Cass told a group of department store executives the secrets of sales success in 1926:

> "Sell them their dreams. Sell them what they longed for and hoped for and almost despaired of having. Sell them hats by splashing sunlight across them. Sell them dreams—dreams of country clubs and proms and visions of what might happen *if only.* After all, people don't buy things to have things. They buy things to work for them. They buy hope—hope of what your merchandise will do for them. *Sell them this hope and you won't have to worry about selling them goods.*"

The early twentieth century social observer William Dean Howells began to realize that the task of the advertiser was not only to tell the truth about a product, but also *"to make the truth sound true."* He must have been the inspiration for Stephen Colbert's brilliant concept, *truthiness.*

And what is the goal of this unceasing clamor of advertising? According to Ernest Elmo Calkins, writing in 1915, "[Advertising] deals with a powerful force called 'public opinion.' This force it creates, controls, and focuses on certain desired ends. These ends are frequently idealistic, requiring a far-reaching vision to grasp and faith to obtain. The effect of such endeavors is beneficial to all—to the public, to the advertiser, to his employee, to the shopkeepers who distribute his goods, and to the conduct of all business."

The *Journal of Political Economy* explained that annoying advertising could be effective advertising.

"The successful advertisement is obtrusive. It continually forces itself upon the attention. It may be on signboards, in the street-car, on the page of a magazine, or on a theater program. Everyone reads it involuntarily, and unconsciously it makes an impression. It is a subtle, persistent, unavoidable presence that creeps into the reader's inner consciousness. A mechanical association is formed and may frequently result in an involuntary purchase."

"...Many people are impressed with the mere fact of advertising. For them, the very obtrusiveness of the advertisement gives social sanction to the value of the article. The more stentorian the voice of the advertiser, the more unquestionably does the purchaser obey."

In the 1947 film, *The Hucksters,* Sidney Greenstreet, playing the role of Evan Llewellyn Evans, president of the Beautee Soap Company, delivers the quintessential speech on the value of intrusive advertising, telling account executive Clark Gable, "Beautee soap, Beautee soap, Beautee soap. Repeat it until it comes out of their ears. Repeat it until they say it in their sleep. Irritate them, Mr. Norman. Irritate, irritate, irritate them."

Evans was based on an actual advertiser, George Washington Hill, president of the American Tobacco Company, whose hard-selling tactics for Lucky Strike cigarettes became legend. Hill insisted on catchy slogans, exaggeration and repetition. He tapped the untouched women's cigarette market with *Reach for a Lucky Instead of a Sweet* campaign touting tobacco as a way to lose weight. Permanently.

Business thought leaders were focused on finding ways to increase consumer demand. The *Journal of Political Economy* went so far as to advocate that consumers literally be trained to want *more,* "In general, education for the lower class must mean the excitation of new wants."

In the same vein, Emily Fogg Meade, a pioneer in sociology (and mother of famed anthropologist Margaret Meade) observed in 1901, "Advertising is a mode of education by which the knowledge of consumable goods is increased."

She elaborated, "He [the advertiser] must excite desire by appealing to imagination and emotion."

In 1912, the social economist Walter Weyl published a book, *The New Democracy,* which noted the power of advertising to create brands. "By advertising, by sheer repetition of a request to buy, manufacturers could directly appeal over the heads of shopkeepers and middlemen to the consumers of the nation. The growing needs of the people were reduced to one common denominator. Individual preferences were accommodated and compromised. The cigarette factories and biscuit factories compelled the people of Los Angeles and Boston of Jacksonville and Duluth to ask for the identical cigarette or biscuit."

Even before the Wright Brothers ever took flight, advertising was seen as the way to build demand and create brands. 1901's *Journal of Political Economy* presented the case history of the Uneeda Biscuit. Note that the brand name, *Uneeda Biscuit,* is a play on phonetics, as it sounds like "you need a biscuit." Could this have been the birth of subliminal advertising?

"There has been no better example of the conditions under which a trust must undertake advertising in order to increase consumption than that of the Uneeda Biscuit. Crackers have never been much advertised. Sales men were extensively used, but methods of advertising, except occasionally to accommodate some dealer, were not employed. The managers of the National Biscuit Company, after completing their organization, found that the capacity of their plants far exceeded the demand for the product."

"An old soda biscuit was put up in a new form under a name [You-Need-A Biscuit] which could be cleverly manipulated. Half a million dollars was spent in advertisements. Sign boards, newspapers, and placards clamored for notice. The success was immediate, and the whole supply was soon exhausted. This advertising is being continued, for otherwise the sales would decrease. Moreover, the trust is now directing the method of distribution to suit its own ends. Consumers are advised of the advantages of the package arrangement with the *In-Er-Seal* in preference to purchasing loose crackers."

Until then, crackers were sold unbranded and packed loosely in barrels. Mothers would give their sons a paper bag and ask them to run down to the store and get the bag filled with crackers.

A typical Uneeda newspaper advertisement from 1905 read:

> If you will eat more
> Uneeda Biscuit
>
> You can do more work
> Enabling you to earn more money,
> So that you can buy more
> Uneeda Biscuit
>
> Do more work and earn still more
> Money

The neat tautology comprised of eating Uneeda biscuits in order to have the energy to earn the money necessary to buy more Uneeda Biscuits is a restatement of mankind's oldest myth, that of the Ouroboros.

I hear you asking, "What the heck is an Ouroboros?"

Trust me, you know the answer to this one. The Ouroboros is that ancient symbol depicting a serpent or dragon swallowing its own tail and paradoxically forming an eternal circle with neither end nor beginning.

The ancient philosopher Plato described a self-eating, circular being as the first living thing in the universe—an immortal, perfectly constructed animal.

Did this forgotten Uneeda Biscuit copywriter know that he was neatly restating the entire cycle of our consumerist/materialist society in his rhyme? Or that he was plagiarizing Plato?

I will admit that when I worked at McCann Erickson I can't recall any of my fellow account executives recounting the Ouroboros myth over an expense account martini. Of course, after a couple of those martinis I certainly was capable of swallowing my own tail.

Paradise in Aisle Eight

This store is the Rainbow and the Pot of Gold.

— John Wanamaker

Look around your supermarket.

Look in your closet.

Look in your medicine cabinet.

Look in your garage.

The Brand Gods are all here — invited or not.

When the gods become brands, their sacred properties are imbued into products and services. So Dionysius finds himself inside a can of Budweiser, and the god of wine becomes The King of Beers. Eros animates the Victoria's Secret retail empire. Our pal Priapus has become Viagra, keeping the magic alive between the sexes.

We can see that brands, through a sort of mission creep, have taken on various characteristics of the ancient gods. Deep down inside, powerful brands and the power of the invisible spirits share some important transcendent DNA.

These ancient and indigenous gods are magical. They make it rain; cause people to fall in love; bring wealth; and even snake a ground ball between the shortstop and third base to win the World Series.

The promise of magical solutions is an essential technique for marketers. Advertising assures that each of us has the power to spin straw into gold. Marketing's magic lamp suggests that the genie of merchandising will be more than happy to grant an unlimited number of wishes.

At the end of the eighteenth century, Sears, Roebuck and Co. became the Aladdin's lamp for all of America with the introduction of the Sears mail order catalog.

That era saw the beginnings of modern marketing and consumer product branding. Pioneering practitioners included Richard Sears and Alvah Roebuck, who realized that America's rural population did not have access to the wealth of products available to city dwellers. This was a time when seventy percent of Americans lived in the countryside; the population was spread far and wide by western migration and the sheer vastness of the American continent; and travel to a major city could take days or even weeks in areas not served by a railroad. Most businesses were small and individually owned.

Rural Americans relied on traveling salesmen and small, local general stores for the goods they wanted. The general store was a part of most rural communities, stocking utilitarian items such as dry goods and sewing supplies, groceries, common tools and a few medicines.

Beginning around 1880, "American business began to create a new set of commercial enticements—a commercial aesthetic—to move and sell goods in volume. This was the core aesthetic of the American capitalist culture, offering a vision of the good life and of paradise," says historian William Leach.

"Cultures must generate some conception of paradise or some imaginative notion of what constitutes the good life. They must bring up a set of images, symbols, and signs that stir up interest at the very least, and devotion and loyalty at the most." American business was happy—then as well as now—to supply its conception of paradise to the masses.

Sears recognized the growing hunger for more and better products in rural America, and set about bringing a consumer paradise to its doorsteps. He recognized that the spreading railroads and the United States Postal Service offered the means to deliver merchandise directly to customers without need for a store or a salesperson. While he did not invent the catalog business, many say he perfected it. By 1895, the Sears & Roebuck catalog included 552 pages, offering a cornucopia of shoes, women's clothing, work clothes, fishing tackle, cook stoves, musical instruments, guns, watches, jewelry, even baby carriages.

The crowded, densely printed pages of the catalog (nicknamed *America's Wish Book*) presented rural Americans with an abundance of goods that promised to make their lives easier, to bring beauty, culture, and sophistication into their country lives.

Against rural traditions of scarcity and self-sufficiency, the Sears catalog projected materialistic consumption as a path to satisfaction and fulfillment. On each page, readers were presented with a variety of readily available, previously unimaginable material goods. . The catalog was a travel guide, presenting a world with streets paved of gold.

In its day, mail order was as miraculous as the Internet has been in ours. Sears Roebuck brought the store (and it was the world's *biggest* store!) right to your kitchen table—wherever that table might be located. The railroad and the US Postal Service were the magic connectors enabling anyone, anywhere, to purchase virtually anything to be shipped anywhere in the United States.

Sears-Roebuck was the dijinni from Aladdin's lamp. Whatever you wished from the Wish Book, it was delivered. The Thousand and One Arabian Nights fairy tale had come true for millions of rural Americans. Mail order was magical!

Our hunger for magical solutions helps to explain why the Harry Potter series—with its Hogwarts School of Witchcraft and Wizardry—has become a runaway best seller. First published in 1997, well over 400 million copies of the Harry Potter books have been sold worldwide.

Today, in fierce competition to recruit a generation of students who grew up on tales of young wizards, a variety of decidedly non-magical colleges and universities have tried to co-brand themselves with enchanted Hogwarts.

As reported in the New York Times by Lauren Edelson, one of those college applicants says: "I drink in the tour guide's every word as he shows my group around Middlebury College's campus. He tells us about the school's new science building and gives us the scoop on nearby ski mountains. I'm about to ask about science research opportunities when he points to a nearby field and mentions the sport students play there: a flightless version of J. K. Rowling's Quidditch game — broomsticks and all."

"I was surprised when many top colleges delivered the same pitch. It turns out they're all a little bit like Hogwarts — the school for witches and wizards in the "Harry Potter" books and movies. Or at least, that's what the tour guides kept telling me."

Dartmouth tour guides boast how its large wood-paneled rooms evoke the atmosphere of Hogwarts. Miss Edelson reports that, at one liberal arts college, students voted to name four buildings on campus after the four houses in Hogwarts: Gryffindor, Ravenclaw, Hufflepuff and Slytherin.

Even at prestigious Harvard, "the admissions officer compared the intramural sports competitions there to the Hogwarts House Cup. The tour guide told me that I wouldn't be able to see the university's huge freshman dining hall as it was closed for the day, but to just imagine Hogwarts' Great Hall in its place." We are urged to pick our college based on its resemblance to the settings in the undeniably magical, but completely fictional, Harry Potter saga.

Fairy tales are especially suited to create a perfect world of desire and wish fulfillment in the mind of consumers. Since fairy tales appeal to the human desires for peace and happiness, they promote consumerism in a society informed by the drive toward instantaneous gratification.

Innovatively employed fairy-tale motifs are ideal for spreading irresistible messages to consumers, suggesting there is a

Fairy Godmother who solves all problems with the magic wand of consumer goods and services.

Such advertisements remind prospects of the fairy tale's happy ending, leading them subconsciously to the conclusion that the product being sold must be equally wonderful.

Take, for example, the elves – *Snap, Crackle,* and *Pop* – who sell Kellogg's Rice Krispies.

The first mention of these elves in a 1933 radio commercial explicitly referenced their fairyland roots: "Listen to the fairy song of health, the merry chorus sung by Kellogg's Rice Krispies as they merrily *snap, crackle, and pop* in a bowl of milk. If you've never heard food talking, now is your chance."

Inspired by the jingle, an illustrator named Vernon Grant sketched out the three characters, which he christened Snap, Crackle, and Pop, and sold his creation to Kellogg's. Grant had no idea his drawings were going to endure as brand imagery for at least the next eighty years. Camille Paglia would note this as an example of how those who create advertising are modern folk artists.

As with Snap, Crackle, and Pop, the Keebler elves who bake all those cookies in a magic tree also began with the lyrics of an advertising jingle. In this case, it was, "Man, you never would believe where the Keebler Cookies come from. They're baked by little elves in a hollow tree. And what do you think makes these cookies so uncommon? They're baked in magic ovens, and there's no factory. Hey!" These lyrics are attributed to Tom Shutter, a copywriter at the Leo Burnett ad agency in 1967.

Chicago's Leo Burnett was the agency best known for creating magical figures to sell consumer products. From the shores of Lake Michigan came brand stalwarts such as The Jolly Green Giant, Kellogg's Tony the Tiger, the Pillsbury Doughboy, and even the Marlboro Man.

Fairy tales enchanted John Wanamaker, leading exponent of consumerism, department store pioneer, and perhaps the most influential merchant before Sam Walton. He wrote fairy stories for his children. Most tellingly, he incorporated fairy tale themes and imagery into his advertising and merchandising.

One of his 1922 advertisements said, "There is a Garden Of Merchandise in Philadelphia...'Is this Wishmakers' Town?' asked a country man entering the front door. 'Yes it is – though some people call it Wanamaker's town'... This store is the Rainbow and the Pot of Gold."

Sears had its *Wish Book.*

Wanamaker's had *Wishmakers' Town.* And a pot of gold.

Wishes were coming true for American consumers. For example:

- Between 1890 and 1910, manufacturing output of pianos increased 500 percent from 72,000 from 370,000, along with an increased output of piano stools, sheet music, and candelabras

- Glassware and lamp manufacturing tripled from 84,000 tons in 1890 to 250,563 tons in 1914

- Manufacturing output of inexpensive jewelry doubled in the decade between 1890 and 1900

The machine was being fed indeed.

The drive to connect the everyday, the *mundane,* to the supernatural is not limited to Americans, of course. Writing in 1954, the French essayist Roland Barthes discusses the newest model of the Citroën automobile, suggesting that its perfection belongs to the realm of fairy-tales.

Before reading what Barthes has to say, remember that he is *French,* and given to shameless intellectual showmanship.

"It is obvious that the new Citroën has fallen from the sky, inasmuch as it appears at first sight as a superlative object. We must not forget that an object is the best messenger of a world above that of nature: one can easily see in an object at once a perfection and an absence of origin, a closure and a brilliance, a transformation of life into matter (matter is much more magical that life), and in a word a *silence* which belongs to the realm of fairy-tales."

BMW claims to be the *ultimate driving machine.* But can BMW compete with a Citroën that has come directly from heaven to our driveway? Such is the power of the brand gods.

Life in BrandLand

We have bought into the idolatrous notion that we are what we buy.

— Tyler Wigg-Stephenson

Once upon a time, we were defined by what we believed, how we worked, where we lived. Now, we are defined by what we own.

"A mere half century ago, it was the producer that the brand legitimized—the origin and authenticity of the product. Today a brand legitimizes the consumer—the individual's and community's origin and authenticity. A brand is no longer a flat sign for corporate identification, a two-dimensional logo plastered on the outside of a bottle. Brands are distinctive markers of human identity," says brand guru Douglas Atkins.

Tyler Wigg-Stephenson adds, "We have bought into the idolatrous notion that we are what we buy…our self-creation via consumption is patent idolatry because it puts transcendent meaning into utterly nontranscendent things…advertising is our common story, communicating that which we hold dear."

Lee Clow, creator of Apple's *Think Different* campaign at TBWA says that brands "articulate who you are and what your values are."

Doug Atkins urges brand managers and their advertising agencies to move beyond product attributes and benefits. He dynamites advertising's sacred concept of the Unique Selling Proposition. "Get an integrated symbolic system. Get over the plastic, the wires, the fillers, and the ingredients. Think about the symbol system you're making possible instead—that is where you'll find true and lasting differentiation."

Referring back to the example of the Apple store, Adkins asks marketers, "What kind of environment are you creating that will allow your customers a place to commune with their fellow believers and the distinct symbols of their belief? *What Temple to what god are you creating?*"

Douglas B. Holt tackles the concept of brands as collective belief systems, "Marketers often like to think of brands as a psychological phenomenon which stem from the perceptions of individual consumers. But what makes a brand powerful is the collective nature of these perceptions; the stories have become conventional and so are continually reinforced because they are treated as truths in everyday interactions."

In 1905, one of John Wanamaker's display managers wrote, "People do not buy the thing, they buy the effect."

Today, that effect often involves the creation or affirmation of a personal identity. The great questions of existentialism have found their answer in materialism.

A founding father of existentialism, the Danish philosopher Søren Kierkegaard wrote, "What I really lack is to be clear in my mind what I am to do, not what I am to know…the thing is to find a truth which is true for me, *to find the idea for which I can live and die.*" Kierkegaard could have solved his existential crisis simply by purchasing a Macintosh computer.

Douglas Atkin describes the Fifth Avenue Manhattan Apple store as a temple to everything Mac. "As you enter, you are faced with a stunning but simple glass staircase. On the first floor there are side chapels dedicated to the worship of digital photography, MP3's, and sleek laptops. Upstairs is the confessional—the Apple bar—where past mistakes are corrected and absolved any software misuse and hardware abuse. Worshippers' doubts are heard and some truths and answers are given here too…ministering quietly and reverentially, are the black clad acolytes, always on hand to explain the doctrine of loading of software or give instructions on downloading music."

Sociologists Albert Muniz and Thomas O'Guinn studied brand communities such as Mac users, discovering that these groups showed "all the traditional markers of sociologically defined groups…[fostering] an intrinsic sense of connection between their members and a collective sense of difference from those not within the community."

Humankind has long identified various groups by their tribal affiliations. We seek to belong to a tribe. We signal that 'belonging' by what we wear, own, consume, watch, and read.

Brands are imbued with stories that customers find useful in constructing their own personal identities. For some, that search for a fundamental truth has led to t-shirts emblazoned *Members Only, North Face, Apple,* and *Harley.*

Charles Darwin postulated that mankind's ability to cooperate led to its remarkable evolutionary success. Those who act in groups have a better chance of overcoming life's challenges. The desire to be part of a group is an archetypal human longing, rooted in pragmatic realism…and a reason why brand tribes can be so appealing.

The evolutionary function of tribes is survival of the group. Members of the tribe share unique attributes, which evolve from their common experiences, knowledge, skills, history, and values. Anthropological accounts of tribes around the world note that tribal members refer to their group as *the people*; by extension, no others are part of *the people*.

Adkins explores the paradox of those who view themselves as strongly individualistic, yet find comfort in belonging to groups. *"Belonging makes me more me*, according to a cult member I interviewed. This paradox was consistently confirmed whether I talked to members of a cult, a social group, or brand community, whether Krishna, Marine, sorority, Trekkie, or Apple addict."

"In a consumer society, successful brands are highly effective in communicating meaning, and *cultic* brands offer self-actualization. That is, they offer us an enhanced and comprehensive version of what we believe ourselves to be."

Adkins advises marketers "instead of trying not to alienate anyone, you must target the alienated and simultaneously separate your organization from the mainstream. Harley-Davidson embraces this approach when its brand guidelines document says, *"Harley is not for everyone."*

Tribal belonging can be signified by something as simple as our choice of beverage, as reported by Michael S. Rosenwald in the Washington Post.

"Luisa Calderon, 28, a radio marketing executive, stood at the bar with her friend, Rossanna Hernandez, 30, a consultant with Ernst & Young. 'Our lives may not be as glamorous as the girls on 'Sex in the City,' "Calderon said. "But that doesn't mean we can't try."

Hernandez agreed: "We can live vicariously through them by drinking nice liquor.'" The women were at a tasting event sponsored by Johnny Walker Gold at Manhattan's Topaz nightclub.

Sometimes the choice is driven by the group, as in "my family always buys Toyota—my dad drank Budweiser and that's what I drink—like mom said, you can never go wrong with Stouffers."

And sometimes the choice is so ingrained as to be both automatic and unconscious—just as our nationality is usually something given to us, and intrinsic to who we are ("I am an American") and the thought of actually changing such an allegiance is profoundly unsettling ("I really can't imagine being a citizen of another country") so the choice of brand can be as deeply anchored.

Time and again, members of brand communities describe their discovery of the chosen brand as a mystical or magical occurrence. "The very first time I heard a Harley-Davidson, I knew I had to have one."

Douglas Atkin writes, "The self story is rewritten and retold to confer significance on what appeared at the time to be a random event. It's as if the meeting [discovery of the chosen brand] must transcend the apparent ordinariness of accident in order to bear the weight of the significance in the person's life that the subsequent events conferred."

In a similar vein, Tyler Wigg-Stephenson, parodying modern evangelism, draws parallels between Jesus and the old door-to-door Fuller Brush salesman. "Behold I stand at the door and knock—the moment of conversion in this depiction is that glorious moment when we deign to let him in, that salvific Fuller Brush man or Mary Kay rep who stand ready to make the sale that will change our lives."

Atkins suggests, "Cult brand marketers know that they must colonize every single moment of everyday life. Their mission is to brand a living *experience*, to create a unified meaning system that transforms every possible touch-point between the company and the customer into symbol that refers back to a single idea or belief. Like a Hare Krishna temple."

Brands such as Harley-Davidson have undeniable *cult appeal*.

Author Douglas Atkin provides us with a look inside Harley-Davidson's official brand guidebook, describing "[The] three essential elements to the Harley-Davidson experience which riders feel for the first time they ride:

1. *The joy of individualism* — the chance to be free, to make choices

2. *The commitment to adventure* — the opportunity to change, to discover new experiences and emotions

3. *The reward of fulfillment* — an intense, persona and consuming bond with the bike that means a richer fuller life

In the language of sociology, these brand guidelines strongly reflect the *social norms* of Harley-Davidson owners.

Social norms are defined as the implicit, or explicit, rules a group has defined for the acceptable behavior, values, and beliefs of its members. Group members who do not accept these rules are rejected by other group members. Social norms determine how you behave in a given situation. The group often very strictly enforces these norms, and offenders are ostracized or rebuked for their conduct.

An academic paper from the Association for Consumer Research exploring the Harley-Davidson mystique says, "Their product draws totemic strength from its link with outlaw counterculture; yet a link that is too tight, i.e., that sullies the company image with the dark side of outlaw bikers, may alienate the upscale market that purchases new Harley-Davidsons."

Authors John W. Schouten and James H. McAlexander describe how Harley-Davidson adapts the social norms of outlaw biker gangs to its branding: "Retained from the outlaw mystique are a sense of brotherhood and outsider status. These are reinforced symbolically by HOG's (*Harley Owner's Group*—a company sponsored group) uniform vest and insignias reminiscent of the outlaw's colors."

Note the emphasis on *outsider status.*

"One manifestation of the Harley mystique that has important implications for merchandising is the extraordinary brand identification to the Harley-Davidson name among motorcycle owners and non-owners alike. For motorcycle owners, Harley licensed products provide a means to include Harley-Davidson symbols in non-riding facets of their lives, serving as reminders to themselves and others that they are part of the Harley brotherhood.

"For one informant, a physician in an upscale clinic, a Harley-Davidson tie tack serves to elicit conversation with patients and peers relating to Harley ownership…for non-owners, Harley licensed products, especially apparel, demonstrate an allegiance to the Harley concept and aspirations to become Harley owners. Although they currently may not be able to afford a Harley-Davidson motorcycle, they can through symbolic identification share in the mystique keep and the dream of ownership alive."

Harley-Davison has inspired books, films, and music. The book *Harley-Davidson and Philosophy* is devoted to exploring the metaphysics of the Harley brand in detail.

Author Bernard E. Rollin describes meeting a fellow Harley rider on the road, "In the first place, the easy camaraderie that our conversation evidenced is typical of what occurs when Harley riders of all backgrounds meet under any circumstance. There is an instant bonding that can be found among fraternity brothers, Shriners, and former New Yorkers. Some of it is, of course, very simply the brotherhood of people evidenced in those who share a common interest. But there is something extra among Harley Riders that is elusive to characterize, but exists nonetheless. It is not only a sense of shared pursuit, but also a kind of quiet elitism stemming from absolute certainty that one is privy to *something that most people will neither experience nor understand."*

Welcome to the tribe.

Creating the Brand Gods

The brand becomes a symbol, a material embodiment of the myth. So as customers drink, drive, or wear the product, they experience a bit of the myth. This is a modern secular example of the rituals that anthropologists have documented in every human society. But rather than religious myths, in modern societies the most influential myths address people's identities.

– Douglas B. Holt

I began my marketing career believing that effective selling involved reasoned, rational appeals to prospective customers. Sure, humor or drama or great design helped to call attention to the core message. But that core message was rational.

Our industry called that ideal rational solution the Unique Selling Proposition.

The legendary advertising executive Rosser Reeves, who worked for Ted Bates and Company in New York, conceived the Unique Selling Proposition, or USP, in the 1940s. Research revealed that top performing advertisements described a specific product benefit that the competition did not offer.

On its face, this is a logical, rational concept.

To be effective, the Unique Selling Proposition had to be communicated with flair via a memorable and easily understood message. Of course, the product benefit had to be important to the customer. There's no use arguing that your aspirin tablets are colored blue. That might be unique, but of no particular benefit to the customer.

Some frequently cited examples of effective Unique Selling Propositions include:

> Anacin: "For fast Fast FAST RELIEF!"

> Domino's Pizza: "Fresh, hot pizza delivered to your door in under 30 minutes—or it's free."

> FedEx: "When your package absolutely, positively has to get there overnight."

At first glance, all seem perfectly logical and rational.

Perhaps.

During my Freshman Anthropology class at the University of Pennsylvania, I learned that members of many indigenous cultures believe that each tree, rock, stream, bird, and bug carries its own spirit.

Members of those tribes believe the magic of the gods is literally everywhere and in everything.

One prays to the spirit of the deer before dining on its flesh; the spirit of the stream is propitiated with offerings of wine before fishing; the ancestors are even thought to aid lost hunters in the woods.

As an 18 year old, I laughed at the foolishness of those indigenous cultures. I also got a C in the course. Served me right.

As I grew older, I learned more about the world.

Late one rainy March night in 1982, just before Saint Patrick's Day, I stopped in a dark tavern on Manhattan's Eighth Avenue. The midnight night crowd thinned until I was the only patron left at the old mahogany bar. The conversation with the barkeep turned to the upcoming St. Patrick's holiday. I chuckled at the cheesy green shamrocks and leering paper leprechaun decorations hanging from the smoke-stained tin ceiling. The Irish bartender put his hand on my arm, and told me to hush up about the wee folk. He spoke softly about the leprechauns and other sprites that lived atop his mother's kitchen cupboards. "Sure as you're sitting on that stool," he assured me.

Psychologist Carl Jung observed these phenomena as well, "In a mythological age these forces were called *mana*, spirits, demons, and gods, and they are as active today as they ever were. If they conform to our wishes, we call them happy hunches or impulses and pat ourselves on the back for being smart fellows. If they go against us, then we say it is just bad luck, or that certain people have it in for us, or it must be pathological. The one thing we refuse to admit is that we are dependent on 'powers' beyond our control."

My father, who piloted B-17 bombers over Europe in World War II, denied every aspect of the supernatural, and spent a lifetime avoiding churches. Dad had no use for Carl Jung's mana. But struggling to bring a crippled bomber home in the April fog over his base in Thurleigh, England, the compass would suddenly point south when the plane was headed north. Empty gasoline tanks appeared full on brand new fuel gauges.

Gremlins were the best explanation for why all of his planning and training seemed futile in the face of cascading equipment failures. "I saw them crawling on the wing, and it wasn't only me who saw them either," he used to say when we talked about the war. He hated gremlins more than he hated Democrats.

Is it coincidence that, when flying from the US to England in early 1945, his plane stopped in Iceland to refuel? The New York Times reports that in Iceland, "Polls consistently show that the majority of the population either believes in elves [known as *alfar* in the Icelandic language] generally described as humanlike creatures who are fiercely protective of their rocky homes—or is not willing to rule out their existence…A belief not just in elves but also in the predictive power of dreams, in the potency of dead spirits and in other supernatural phenomena, is closely linked to Iceland's Celtic traditions."

Could those gremlins have been hitchhiking Icelandic elves?

I tried to explain the concept of these lesser gods who animate our world to my skeptical friend, and baseball fanatic, Rich, at a Memorial Day picnic where our kids were playing softball. Rich scoffed at the notion that any rational man would believe such foolishness.

Seeking a compelling example, I asked him, "You know how a batter threads a hit into the gap between third base and the shortstop in baseball?"

"Of course," he replied. "Sweetest play there is. Sometimes it seems impossible, but the ball just slips invisibly right through the gap."

"Ever listen to the play-by-play announcer?"

"Of course."

"Ever hear him say, 'Wow! That ball had eyes.'"

"Yep."

"Get my point?"

"Yep."

That was probably the first time Rich ever agreed with Carl Jung.

Even the eminent economist John Maynard Keynes turned to invisible spirits to explain the behavior of the marketplace. "Most, probably, of our decisions to do something positive, the full consequences of which will be drawn out over many days to come, can only be taken as the result of *animal spirits*—a spontaneous urge to action rather than inaction, and not as the outcome of a weighted average of quantitative benefits multiplied by quantitative probabilities."

Sort of like that ball snaking between shortstop and second base. Or a compass suddenly confused about which was south and which was north.

Such invisible energies have been outwardly banished from modern society. Our dominant monotheistic religions do not recognize the existence of lesser spirits. And a predominant belief in the *scientific method* demands objective measurable evidence and repeatable results rather than gremlins. In our now *rational* universe, we are not often permitted to either honor or acknowledge those spirits directly.

A primal memory of that enchanted world lives on in our marketplace. Carl Jung says this is part of our unconscious representing the collective memory of all humanity's past held inside the unconscious mind. Jung would have loved the concept of crowdsourcing.

Once I got over my resistance to Anthropology 101, I noticed that my own neighborhood was full of people who, desperate to sell their houses, buried statues of St. Joseph upside down in the front yard. Some houses bore hex signs borrowed from the Amish to ward off the evil eye. My own mother, raised in Alabama, insisted that my family must eat black-eyed peas with pork every New Year's day for luck. Some of my Jewish neighbors nailed a mezuzah to their doorframes as proof of their faith.

Belief in the supernatural is as American as apple pie. Of course, the smell of apples, long a staple of sorcery, played a role in the Salem witch trials, helping to point the community finger of vindication at the evildoers.

Jackson Lears describes Americans' traditional reliance on the supernatural, writing in *Fables of Abundance*. "Caught between their own experience of scarcity and the achievement ethos of a developing entrepreneurial society, they sought economic self-transformation through collaboration with supernatural powers."

"In the United States, treasure seeking through occult means was an obsessive and widespread preoccupation well into the nineteenth century, especially in poorer rural regions where people felt left behind by economic development. American treasure seekers used seer stones, divining rods, and other occult paraphernalia in a busy scientific spirit, assembling empirical evidence and following precise procedures."

Googled: The End Of The World As We Know It opens with a description of a 2003 visit by Mel Karmazin, CEO of the media conglomerate Viacom, to meet with top Google executives. Most media, such as magazines and TV shows, rely on an advertising revenue model that depends on salesmanship, emotion, and mystery. "You buy a commercial on the Super Bowl, you're going to pay two and a half million dollars for the spot," Karmazin told the Google team. "I have no idea if it's going to work. You pay your money, you take your chances." The Gods of Advertising determine who wins and who loses in that game.

Then the Google team explained how its *AdSense* advertising model delivered precisely targeted messages to defined audiences, with the ability to track the effectiveness of every dollar spent.

That was not the world Karmazin came from. He exclaimed to the Google team,

"You're fucking with the magic!"

But can the magic be entirely removed?

Winged Mercury no longer speeds from place to place faster than the wind. But even now, out on some two lane blacktop west of Laramie, the spirit of Mercury animates a lone Harley-Davidson rider, lean and rangy, racing into the red horizon of a Wyoming twilight (credit here to the Jordan Motor Car Company and its legendary 1923 ad, *"Somewhere west of Laramie"*).

Our motorcyclist roars past a roadside cliff face, where a thousand years ago a Native American shaman chipped the image of a dancing flute player into the rock. This is Kokopelli, a prehistoric spirit of prosperity and fertility, who dances and plays his flute to this day, offering a silent blessing to the passing man on the wheeled pony.

A rock is simply a rock—until the petroglyph carved into the cliff is recognized as representing the eternal spirit who lives within, animating the inanimate.

If a rock is just a rock, then coffee is just a cup of Joe—until the Starbucks brand transforms hot water into liquid gold thanks to the magic of hand-roasted, fair-trade, shade-grown coffee beans. Instead of spinning all that straw, a modern Rumplestilskin could ask Rapunzel to simply brew a cup of French roast.

Brands aspiring to become contemporary classics must succeed on many levels. First and foremost, the product needs integrity, and some special quality that sets it apart. Having a story to tell fixes a brand's identity in people's imagination and gets across what it stands for is crucial. The best advertising functions as mythology.

Whether the story is made up or rooted in fact is beside the point. What matters is that the brand's mythology has the power to intrigue and to draw people in.

Contemporary America is short on myth. Our times are devoid of ritual and mysticism. We do not study the Greek classics, whose stories and gods are the foundation of western civilization. A hundred years ago, every student of literature and every college graduate was familiar with Aphrodite, Dionysus, Athena, Hermes, and Artemis. No more. We have lost the stories that define who we are, where we came from, what we value, and what makes us moral.

This is a profound loss. Is it any wonder that books such as the Harry Potter series and *Percy Jackson & The Olympians*, with their tales of magic and ancient gods, captivate today's mythologically starved children?

Carl Jung underscored the essential importance of myths, "Anthropologists have often described what happens to a primitive society when its spiritual values are exposed to the impact of modern civilization. Its people lose the meaning of their lives, their social organization disintegrates, and they themselves morally decay. We are now in the same condition."

Joseph Campbell adds, "Throughout the inhabited world, in all times and under every circumstance, the myths of man have flourished; and they have been the living inspiration of whatever else may have appeared out of the activities of the human body and mind. It would not be too much to say that myth is the secret opening through which the inexhaustible energies of the cosmos pour into human cultural manifestation."

"The wonder is that the characteristic efficacy to touch and inspire deep creative centers dwells in the smallest nursery fairy tale—as the flavor of the ocean is contained in a droplet of the whole mystery of life within the egg of a flea. For the symbols of mythology are not manufactured— they cannot be ordered, invented, or permanently suppressed. They are spontaneous productions of the psyche, and each bears within it, undamaged, the germ power of its source."

"In the absence of an effective general mythology, each of us has his private, unrecognized, rudimentary, yet secretly potent pantheon of dream. The latest incarnation of Oedipus, the continued romance of Beauty and the Beast, stand this afternoon on the corner of Forty Second Street and Fifth Avenue, waiting for the traffic light to change," suggests Campbell.

Brands step into the void created by the lack of an effective societal mythology. The human psyche is hungry for the order and meaning which myth provides. Brands are more than happy to offer up their own vision of how life should be lived. This is one of the secrets of successful consumer marketers.

In the lack of pervasive cultural myths, *Just Do It* becomes a profound philosophical statement.

"Storytelling is the way that communities share and preserve their heritage. Stories explain the nature of organizational life and sustain knowledge. It is through stories that a culture is built…" says Douglas Holt. "Over time, as the brand performs its myth, the audience eventually perceives that the myth resides in the brand's markers (e.g. its name, logo, and design elements)."

"The brand becomes a symbol, a material embodiment of the myth. So as customers drink, drive, or wear the product, they experience a bit of the myth. This is a modern secular example of the rituals that anthropologists have documented in every human society. But rather than religious myths, in modern societies the most influential myths address people's identities." Brands can become a source of existential assurance.

Randall Rothenberg writes, "To succeed, advertising cannot seek to invent a new soul. Instead, it must reinforce and redirect the existing image. It must serve as a form of mythology, providing the corporation's various and often competing constituencies—of which consumers are only one of many— heroes, villains, principles, rules of conduct and stories with which they can rally the faithful to remain true to the cause. Only then, with luck and effort, can they win new converts."

Our myths are increasingly created from what we buy. And what is sold to us.

Jung, for his part, bemoaned that modern society had "stripped all things of their mystery and numinosity; nothing is holy any longer." Paglia would argue that we find such holiness in our brands.

As advertisers create brand gods to fit the immutable archetypes that drive us all, the market takes on characteristics of religion. The marketer seeks to tame the marketplace through incantations of value propositions and brand attributes.

Former Subaru of American President George Miller explained how the company built a brand myth, "It starts with the image we have, and it has a little bit of the flavor of the culture of our business, too. And some of our culture goes all the way back to the engineers who designed the product, and why they designed it the way they did."

Randall Rothenberg echoes Miller when describing the role of an advertising agency president during a new business presentation, "he asserts both his magical powers and his scientific prowess."

Rothenberg describes Subaru of America's search for a new advertising agency. "That's what SOA [Subaru of America] wanted: a new American myth, an Idea so Big that it would immediately integrate Subaru into the collective national consciousness, where already lived George Washington, Babe the Blue Ox, and Snap, Crackle, Pop."

"If big enough, Subaru's Big Idea would be a golden highway at the end of which the company's new image (whatever it might be) would be as shining and memorable as Oz, an icon of wonderment with four wheels and a dash." Subaru was, in fact, looking for that fairy tale magic that Roland Barthes ascribed to the Citroën which had descended in silence from heaven.

Atkins quotes a religious cult member who says, "Belonging allows the individual to become more himself. You become more you." The most powerful brands often have a cult-like pull on their customers.

This flies in the face of popular wisdom that says fans or cult members must lose their individuality. In actuality, fanatics feel a greater sense of their own authenticity, their own individuality, values, and value. This is the paradox of belonging.

The more loyal to the group, the greater the sense of *self-actualization*, because shared myths contribute to an ancient connection between the visible and invisible worlds.

Carl Jung said, "Man positively needs general ideas and convictions that will give a meaning to his life and enable him to find a place for himself in the universe...a sense of a wider meaning to one's existence is what raises a man beyond mere getting and spending. If he lacks this sense, he is lost and miserable."

Jung continues, "Myths go back to the primitive storyteller and his dreams, to men moved by the stirring of their fantasies. These people were not very different from those whom later generations called poets or philosophers." Or copywriters.

"The easiest way to get a meaning system for your brand is to tack on to an existing community's value system," says Doug Atkins. "Your brand...should become a public symbol for the meaning of this group. They should *feel* that it stands for them." An essential part of the Unique Selling Proposition is finding ways to bond the buyer to the brand's value system. For example, Ben & Jerry's ice cream enjoys great loyalty because of the political meaning now implicit in that brand.

Advertising writer Douglas B. Holt postulates that certain brands inhabit particular geographies, which he calls *populist worlds*. These populist worlds, such as *Marlboro Country*, or the Mexican beach where Corona beer is found, are separate from mundane life and the everyday restrictions of society.

The inhabitants of these populist worlds act as they desire, not as they are required by rules or authority. When customers identify with these populist worlds, they become citizens of an alternative brand universe.

The Marlboro smoker becomes a cowboy—tough, wise, independent.

The Corona drinker is on a perpetual beach holiday—freed from the constrictions of the 9-to-5 world.

The Harley-Davidson rider is an outlaw—following his own code of justice, secure in his ability to take care of himself.

The transformation is magical. At my church, the priest quotes Jesus at Communion, saying, "Eat this, this is my body given to you."

That's not far off from Corona suggesting, "Drink me, and cast aside your BlackBerry."

Of course, Walt Disney worked this wizardry better than anyone—by actually creating a magical country named Disneyland! The man, the brand, the land...all in service of your fantasy.

Today even real nations with centuries of art, culture, history, and heritage such as China and France fight for the right to have a Disneyland grafted onto their own geography. This is the power of brand to conjure entire worlds, galaxies, eternities of imagining and meaning—and immense water slides.

In her essay, *The Myth of Authenticity,* Alicia Clegg explores how marketers create these populist worlds. She begins, "Somewhere in my handbag there's a bar of chocolate with mysterious links to ancient Mayans. I'm going to eat it with a mug of coffee from the volcanic slopes and Caribbean mountains of Guatemala. My diet may not be good for me, but it's loaded with interesting background details."

Clegg continues, "Working the link between place of origin and product quality is the oldest trick in the brand book. It milks our thirst for mythology and plays mercilessly on our superstitious hope that special places have the power to revitalize and transform."

Many of these brands relying on the *mystique of place* are entirely, or at least partially, works of fiction. What she calls trickster brands include Häagen Dazs, the American super-premium ice cream, which when launched implied that its heritage was Danish. What could be more Danish than "Häagen" with its umlaut and extended "ahh" sound?

But wait. Wikipedia tells us that "Häagen-Dazs is a brand of ice cream, established by *Polish immigrants* Reuben and Rose Mattus in the Bronx, New York, in 1961. The name does not derive from any of the North Germanic languages; it is simply two made-up words meant to look Scandinavian to American eyes (the digraphs *äa* and *zs* are not a part of any native words in any of the Scandinavian languages)."

This is known in the marketing industry as foreign branding. Mattus knew that Denmark was known for its dairy products and had a positive image in the U.S. He included an outline map of Denmark on early labels to enhance the illusion.

The Häagen Dazs unique selling proposition connected the purchaser to a totally mythical place and culture. Truthiness, anyone?

I am told in deepest confidence by a former Häagen Dazs employee that Reuben Mattus once thought he had a deal to sell his proprietary ice cream formula to the Duncan Hines company. When, at the last minute, Duncan Hines pulled out of the agreement, Mattus thought about naming his product *Hines Duncan* to get even. From that grudge came the Häagen Dazs nomenclature which, at the least, retained the first initials of Hines Duncan.

Another path on the road to faux-authenticity is the creation of a fictional brand personification.

Amanda Hesser, writing in the New York Times Magazine, tells us, "Betty Crocker was the first great supermarket icon. She made baking seem not just satisfying but also necessary to a healthy family life, and she later, in the 1950's, was at the forefront in the convenience movement—Betty was the brainchild of Samuel Gale and James Quint, who in 1921 created her to be the chief of correspondence for Gold Medal flour and to lend a softer image to what was essentially a flour mill in Minnesota."

Susan Marks, in her book *Finding Betty Crocker,* writes that the top executives at Gold Medal thought the name Betty sounded cheery, wholesome, and folksy. The surname Crocker came from William G. Crocker, former director of the Washburn Crosby Company, which owned Gold Medal flour.

Betty Crocker first appeared as a matronly figure whose job it was to advocate that baking cakes at home elevated the status and desirability of clever housewives. Betty Crocker responded to baking questions mailed in by home cooks, and grew into a well-known voice on national radio shows and, later, an image of the ideal housewife on television. In 1945,

Fortune magazine named Betty Crocker the second most popular American woman. Eleanor Roosevelt was named first.

Says Hesser, "By the 90's, her image had been changed to a computer-generated composite of the 75 winners of the Spirit of Betty Crocker contest—prim, conservatively dressed and wearing the expression of someone dosed up on happy pills—someone who pushes mixes, prepackaged icings and convenience foods." Today, you'll find @*BettyCrocker* serving up baking tips on Twitter, and she has over one million Facebook friends!

The Betty Crocker unique selling proposition connects its buyers to a woman who never existed, but whose mythology enshrines an American ideal of the good wife as a great cook.

Betty Crocker has been joined by many other faux-brand personifications—from Aunt Jemima to Uncle Ben, and even that fictional Quaker of oatmeal fame.

The American painter Nina Katchadourian created a 30-foot wide mural, *The Genealogy of the Supermarket,* portraying an imaginary family tree for great American brands. "In Nina Katchadourian's world, the Jolly Green Giant is married to the Indian maiden on Land O' Lakes butter and Little Debbie is sister to the Charmin baby. Mr. Clean and the Brawny Man are now partners and have adopted the Gerber Baby," wrote the New York Times.

The Times continued that the only sour note in Katchadourian's mural was Betty Crocker, "who languishes in a collateral branch married to a man on the Nescafe coffee jar. She should really preside at the top, as the matriarch of the entire clan. Betty Crocker was the first great supermarket icon.

She made baking seem not just satisfying but also necessary to a healthy family life, and she later, in the 1950s, was at the forefront in the convenience movement that bore so many of her descendants on this family tree."

I think Betty Crocker should have married the Marlboro Man.

That nicotine-stained personification of American Anglo-Saxon macho defined a lifestyle, an ethos, and a nation— *Marlboro Country.*

Philip Morris & Co. (now Altria) originally introduced the Marlboro brand as a woman's cigarette in 1924. Filters were added to Marlboro in the 1950s, which only reinforced its image as a cigarette for women. And the Marlboro slogan, "Mild as May," did little to appeal to men.

Advertising legend Leo Burnett sought a radical way to reposition Marlboro to expand its market. Inspiration struck when, in 1947, Life Magazine published a photo essay on modern cowboys—and a photo of real-life Clarence Hailey Long. He was an authentic working cowboy shown in black and white, sunburned, with a three-day beard, cowboy hat, and cigarette in his mouth. Marlboro found its mythic macho mojo.

The Marlboro Man campaign began in 1955. By 1957, sales had increased 300%. The Marlboro unique selling proposition offered men an escape to a Peter Pan world without women, governed by masculine values.

While a number of different models portrayed the Marlboro man over the years, the iconic archetype of the man's man whose persona was embodied in that cigarette hanging out of his mouth was constant. Philip Morris chose another real life cowboy, Darrell Winfield, to be the face of Marlboro into the 1980's.

The magic, of course, was that by lighting up a Marlboro any man became that uber-cowboy, the embodiment of masculinity, power, and sex appeal. The Marlboro Man became the Marlboro Myth, woven into the fabric of American folklore. Don't tell anyone he was born not in Montana, but on Madison Avenue.

In 1991 Don Johnson and Mickey Rourke co-starred in a film titled *Harley Davidson and the Marlboro Man.* Mickey's character was named Harley Davidson, while Don Johnson was the Marlboro Man. A match made in brand heaven, the movie's writer, Don Michael Paul, is no stranger to advertising, having appeared in some fifty TV commercials. He used existing brand imagery to create two character archetypes. Maybe he was really the first to create Brand-Driven Fiction?

Makes you wonder if he's working on a romantic comedy titled *Betty Crocker and the Häagen Dazs Guy.*

Let's revisit those examples of successful Unique Selling Propositions, but view them through the lens of our indigenous tribal friends.

Anacin:

"For fast Fast FAST RELIEF!" This is really the ancient promise of a miracle cure. Make an appeal to the spirit of Anacin, and, miraculously, your headache will go away. Quickly.

Domino's Pizza:

"Fresh, hot pizza delivered to your door in 30 minutes or less—or it's free." Make the proper incantation to Domino, the god of Pizza, and within half an hour a piping hot, ready to eat, pizza of your choice will be delivered by a winged messenger (ok, it's a guy in a Hyundai, but what the heck…) directly to YOUR door. All Domino's asks is a small cash tribute—which will be waived should the god fail to respond to your summons in 30 minutes or less. It's a MIRACLE!

FedEx:

"When your package absolutely, positively has to get there overnight." If the god Domino has some powerful mojo, he pales in comparison to the great sacred FedEx. Time and distance disappear when FedEx struts his stuff. FedEx will take your package *anywhere*, door-to-door, overnight. This is the stuff of Winged Mercury, the messenger of the gods, made real for every one.

Perhaps inside every Unique Selling Proposition is a leprechaun or Icelandic elf, secretly channeling an *Unseen Supernatural Promise*. So long as it is not one of those damn gremlins.

How To Create A Brand— Or Start A Religion

Brands are the new religion.

– Douglas Atkins

By now I know you are asking, "Ok, smarty pants, so now we know about branding. But how can we create a brand? Can anyone do it? Is there a secret?"

Yes, there is a secret. Actually, there are three secrets to creating a powerful brand.

And since this book explores how brands have taken on many of the tasks that the ancient gods once handled for us, stick around and you'll learn how the principles of brand creation can be applied to the creation of new religions.

Here are the three secrets to creating an effective brand, taken from the pages of The Economist Publishing Company's highly regarded book *Brands and Branding*.

You will note that *The Economist* does not mention gods, brand gods, magic, myths, or invisible spirits. After all, it is a British company.

We will fix that soon. Creating a brand and founding a religion are essentially the same process. But the religion is tax deductible, of course.

How to Create a Brand

1. The first of the three secrets to creating a great brand is, "A brand **needs** *a compelling idea.*"

   The Economist blokes say that behind *every brand is a compelling idea that captures consumers' attention and loyalty by filling an unmet or unsatisfied need.* This actually makes sense when you consider you probably won't buy something you don't think you need. That is why marketers appeal to deep, fundamental, psychic needs, such as the longing to be loved, to be strong, to be wealthy, to have superior social status, or to buy hamburgers from a circus clown.

2. The second of the big brand secrets is, "A brand needs a *resolute core purpose* and supporting values."

   I told you these Economist guys were Brits. That's why they use words such as *resolute.* So the *resolute* core purpose of BMW is to create outstanding automobiles ("The Ultimate Driving Machine"); FedEx is *resolute* about accelerating the physical delivery of goods; Nike is *resolute* in its mission to help us perform athletically higher, faster, stronger; Starbucks *resolutely* seeks to satisfy our need to pay ever-increasing prices for caffeine.

3. Which brings us to the last of the three Jedi branding secrets, "A brand needs *a central organizing principle.*"

I know that a *Central Organizing Principle* sounds like the top person at your old high school. Not so.

This Central Organizing Principle refers to the *one idea* around which everything in the brand revolves. For example, the central organizing principle of Wal-Mart is to dominate as the low price leader. Every decision at Wal-Mart has to pass through the filter of "Will this help us grow market share by lowering our prices?" This filter works for every purchase, from tractor-trailers to toilet paper. The brand position, purpose, and values are employed as management levers to guide decision-making. This becomes so ingrained in leading organizations that they consciously ask themselves, "How will this decision impact upon the brand?" or "Will this cause shoppers to trample security guards to death on Black Friday?"

This is all very logical, and perhaps even formulaic. Take a bit of compelling idea, mix in a dash of resolute core purpose (with supporting values), and top it all off with a generous dollop of central organizing principle. Voila! Le Brand!

Now, let's see how this same formula can create a religion.

We will perform a variation of *find and replace,* where the concept of Brand is replaced by the concept of Religion in The Economist magazine recipe for baking a brand.

How to Create a Religion

1. First, a religion needs *a compelling idea.*

    Behind every *religion* is a compelling idea that captures [consumers'] attention and loyalty by filling an unmet or unsatisfied need. (Jesus saves, Allah is great, Oy Vey, etc.)

2. Secondly, a *religion* needs a **resolute core purpose** and supporting values.

   For example, the resolute core purpose of Christianity is salvation. And to sell lots of toys at Christmastime is a supporting value.

3. Finally, a *religion* **needs a central organizing principle.**

   Christianity says Jesus will forgive our sins and provide eternal life. Jews consider mitzvah, the divine commandments, as the key to a good life. Islam believes in happiness through total submission to the will of Allah. The Church of Nike suggests *Just Do It*, while at various times the Temple of Coke has taught that *Coke Adds Life*, and *Coke Is It!* and that we should *Open Happiness*.

I hear the more skeptical readers muttering that the words above have been crassly manipulated to support the author's bias. While crass word manipulation is the author's inherent prerogative, I admit to no such chicanery.

Instead, I refer you to one of modern advertising's founding fathers, Bruce Barton. Among many pioneering advertising accomplishments, Barton and his legendary advertising agency BBD&O is credited with popularizing Betty Crocker in the years after World War I.

Naomi Klein tells us, "In 1923 [adman Bruce Barton] said that the role of advertising was to *help corporations find their soul.* The son of a preacher, he drew on his religious upbringing for uplifting messages—Institutions have souls just as men and nations have their souls, he told GM President Pierre du Pont."

No less an authority than the 1901 *Journal of Political Economy* invoked the transcendent nature of materialism, "Consumption goods on the other hand are bought to *minister* directly to personal satisfaction. The criterion of their worth is the personal enjoyment which they afford. This enjoyment is not purely physical. It contains a spiritual element."

Randall Rothenberg describes the scene as Wilder Baker, the president of one of the shops competing for the Subaru account, introduces his agency's presentation. Baker goes into a dissertation on the soul of a product, the soul of a car. Quoting Socrates, he explains that the soul of a product exists independently of consumers, of manufacturers and advertisers.

Socrates, who might have made a great account executive on Madison Avenue, said, "On the one hand, we have that which is divine, immortal, indestructible, of a single form, accessible to thought, ever constant and abiding true to itself...on the other hand, we have that which is human, mortal, destructible, of many forms." The implication was that the advertising man, the philosopher-king of commercial culture, could, like Socrates himself, bring forth the deepest manifestation of the essence, the Form, the *eidos,* the soul of Subaru. As this idea evolved, Rothenberg suggested that the adman ceased to see himself as a pitchman and instead saw himself as "the philosopher-king of commercial culture."

Randall Rothenberg invokes the ancient Eleusinian Mysteries when describing the behavior of highly regarded brand consultants, "Like the priestesses of Eleusis, they speak in tongues and writhe in ecstasy, their devotions granting them entrée to a higher realm of knowledge..."

One of Barton's predecessors in the world of advertising, Elbert Hubble, literally embraced advertising as his true faith. Hubbard said, "There is room in business for all your religion, all your poetry, all your love...When I want to hear a really good sermon nowadays, we attend a weekly lunch of the ad club, and listen to a man who deals in ways and means and is intent upon bringing about paradise, here and now."

From Hubble's perspective, advertising actually did religion one better, by suggesting that there is no reason to wait to get to heaven—thanks to materialism and consumptionism, heaven had come to earth.

Bruce Barton himself was concerned with the souls of men, along with the corporate soul. Barton took on Jesus as his client.

His book, *The Man Nobody Knows,* first published in 1925, was a modern biography of Jesus which achieved worldwide fame. Barton sought to rectify what he considered the sissified image of Jesus presented in Sunday schools. As Barton's new testament, Jesus was a go-getting young executive who "picked up twelve men from the bottom ranks of business and forged them into an organization that conquered the world."

Contemporary critics thought Barton's portrayal of Jesus made religion seem too much a business—or business too much a religion. But the critics were a small minority. *The Man Nobody Knows* topped popular best-seller lists for two years.

In 1942, Harvard researcher Neil H. Borden published a comprehensive text on advertising effectiveness. *The Economic Effects of Advertising* reported no real impact on demand, or distribution costs, or production costs, or price competition as a result of advertising.

Which begs the question, why are billions of dollars spent every year on traditional advertising, whose effects are difficult, if not impossible, to ascertain? Remember, this has nothing to do with digital advertising, where every click of the mouse is tracked and assigned a monetary value. Traditional advertising, as Mel Karmazin pointed out, is more an act of faith than of science.

Rothenberg writes, "unable to rely on factual proof of advertising's specific powers, Subaru and the six agencies vying for its account were grounding their belief that a new image would lead the auto company into the Jerusalem of renewed prosperity on one principle, *faith.*"

"There was nothing novel in their near-religious certitude. The notion of advertising as the only faith in a secularized consumer society has long antecedents, going back at least as far as Bruce Barton (a founder of BBDO) and his contention that Jesus was the world's greatest ad man. Many scholars have remarked on the similarities between the hortatory style of ads and preachers, between the fantastical dogma of both marketing and organized religion, between the reverence devout acolytes show towards

St. John and the Lubavitcher Rebbe, on the one hand, and to Burnett and Bernbach on the other—Wilder Baker [one of the participants in a Subaru marketing meeting] spoke for all of them when he casually described Subaru's as-yet undiscovered new image. He called it *the grail*."

Naomi Klein suggests, "The search for the true meaning of brands—or the *brand essence,* as it is often called—gradually took the advertising agencies away from individual products and their attributes and toward a psychological/anthropological examination of what brands mean to the culture and to people's lives." This gets closer to that faith which drove the Subaru agency search.

Emile Durkheim, one of the founders of sociology, sought to understand the role and function of religion in general, without paying attention to any of the beliefs or tenets of any particular religion. He was looking at the archetype of religion, seeking to know its universal timeless essence. From our perspective, his work is very relevant for understanding the function and the power of brands.

Durkheim was deeply interested in understanding what held complex modern societies together. Religion, he argued, was an expression of social cohesion. I postulate that if brands have become gods, then brands can equally be expressions of social cohesion.

Durkehim wrote, "For we know today that a religion does not necessarily imply symbols and rites, properly speaking, or temples and priests. This whole exterior apparatus is only the superficial part. Essentially, it is nothing other than a body of collective beliefs and practices endowed with a certain authority."

Durkheim saw totemism as the most basic form, or element, of religion.

The totem, usually an animal or other natural figure, spiritually represents a group of related people such as a clan. Totemism was a key element of study in the development of 19th and early 20th century theories of religion, and, especially for Émile Durkheim, who concentrated his study on indigenous societies.

Observing the identification of social groups with spiritual totems in Australian aboriginal tribes, Durkheim theorized that all human religious expression was intrinsically founded in the relationship to a group.

Replace the concept of totem with *logo* or *brand*, and these constructs hold up equally well.

The British social anthropologist Evans-Pritchard argued that totems were metaphoric. His work with an African tribe called the Nuer led him to believe that totems are a symbolic representation of the group. Had Evans-Pritchard done his fieldwork in Sturgis, ND, he would have seized on the Harley-Davidson logo as the representation for the Harley Nation.

It is in this totemic belief system that the fundamental separation between the *sacred* and the *profane* is most clear. *We* who worship the totem are sacred. All others are profane.

To see the sacred and the profane at work in a branded consumerist society, simply ask a Mac owner to work on an IBM PC. The Mac owner will make a face, and say, "I hate those things. I feel like a dork."

All religions, Durkheim said, are outgrowths of this distinction, adding to it myths, images, and traditions. The totemic animal, [logo/brand] Durkheim believed, was the expression of the sacred—because it was the emblem for a social group, the clan. Religion is thus an inevitable, just as society is inevitable when individuals live together as a group.

And if religion is the inevitable outcome of any society or a group, then *Brand Gods* may be the inevitable outcome of a consumerist society.

Social critic S. Samuel Strauss, writing in The Villager newspaper in June, 1923, observed that "for more than a century *things* have little by little been filling the stream of existence, little by little absorbing the place normally held by the imponderables, by religion, by art and culture. The fact is that capital's appetite for profits, meeting no restraint, has been literally eating its way into out right existence and throwing it all out of proportion." Materialism is not a modern invention.

Durkheim thought that the model for relationships between people and the supernatural was the relationship between individuals and the community. Durkheim believed that people ordered the physical world, the supernatural world, and the social world according to similar principles.

He is famous for suggesting that "God is society, writ large." In a society dominated by brand culture, *God*™ becomes a logo.

And, of course, in our consumerist society, the Brand Gods can easily slip into the pantheon of the other supernaturals.

Durkheim defined the four major functions of religion:

1. Disciplinary—forcing or administrating discipline

2. Cohesive—bringing people together, a strong bond

3. Vitalizing—to make livelier or vigorous, vitalise, boost spirit

4. Euphoric—creating good feeling, happiness, confidence, well-being

Durkheim's four functions are spot-on. And they work equally well to define the attributes of branding:

Disciplined—The discipline is in how the brand elements are consistently orchestrated, in terms of logo, color, form, style and voice, and also in terms of brand loyalty. The great god Kellogg intones, *Thou Shalt Have No Other Frosted Flakes Than Kellogg.* And, behold, little Johnny will eat nothing but Kellogg's Frosted Flakes with Tony the Tiger for breakfast.

Cohesive—Bringing like-minded people together, such as Harley riders or Apple users or COSTCO shoppers, into vast tribal communities.

Vitalizing—Boosting the spirits, as Nike does for athletes, and Jose Cuervo beer does for those craving a break from the daily grind.

Euphoric—What brings good feelings better than Coke (at least if you are buying one for the entire world), or the confidence that comes from having stayed at a Holiday Inn Express last night?

Amen.

Making Magic—Logos and Volvos

There was a time when the Catholic Church sanctioned placing statues and medals of Saint Christopher on automobile dashboards to protect their occupants.

Christopher is the patron saint of travelers. Medallions with his name and image are frequently displayed in automobiles.

Many legends surround St. Christopher, who lived in the third century. Most of them involve a strong warrior named Offero who, after many adventures, converts to Christianity and becomes the companion of a Jesus-worshipping hermit. The hermit tells Offero to devote his life to the service of Christ by using his great strength to help pilgrims cross a very dangerous river. This he does for many years, preventing hundreds of travelers from drowning.

One day a child appears, asking for help crossing the river. Offero places the child on his shoulder and crosses the river—but with every step the child grows heavier and heavier. Offero barely makes it to the other side. The child says to him, "I am so heavy because I bear the weight of the world." With that, the Christ-child baptizes Offero with his new name, Christopher, which means "Christ bearer."

In France, travelers are advised to "Regarde Saint Christophe et va-t-en rassuré" (Look at Saint Christopher and go on reassured). Having driven on French roads, I doubt any such assurances would bring comfort.

Spain's Saint Christopher medals and holy cards bear the phrase "Si en San Cristóbal confías, de accidente no morirás" ("If you trust St. Christopher, you won't die in an accident"). That might be a good slogan for the insurance-selling gecko.

This Saint Christopher must have been the Ralph Nader of his day, which was around 225 AD in what was to become Germany—future home of the BMW and Mercedes brands. Saint Chris was ahead of his time.

Saint Christopher's feast day was removed from the official Roman Catholic calendar of saints in 1969, as verified evidence of his life and his work was deemed inadequate. Even great religions are falling prey to the rational world's demand for scientific evidence of their own saints! I wonder if Mel Karmazin would tell the Pope that he's fucking with the magic?

With St. Christopher banned from league play, where was a fearful traveler to find reassurance against the possibility of death-by-motor-crash? And what of the millions of St. Christopher medallions which had suddenly lost their mojo?

Fortunately, a couple of Swedish engineers were ready to step up to the plate.

Assar Gabrielson and Gustaf Larson set out to create an automobile company guided by one overarching principle—that since cars are driven by people, and carry friends and families, they would build the safest cars available.

Then they invented the Volvo.

Volvo has indeed been true to the spirit of safety, pioneering such innovations as the laminated windshield in 1944, the three-point safety belt in 1959, the rear facing child safety seat in 1972, and the side impact air bag in 1994. I am certain that St. Christopher would be proud—if maybe a bit jealous.

In another instance of accidental branding, the word *Volvo* has nothing to do with safety or Catholic saints. It comes from the Latin verb meaning "to roll." Volvo joins eBay and Starbucks as great brand names whose original meaning had nothing to do with what they came to signify.

Volvo's magic extends even further, according to the shirt that reads, "Practice Safe Sex. Make Love In A Volvo."

The Volvo logo is a circle with a short arrow pointing up and to the right. This was the ancient Roman symbol for the planet Mars, which represented the god of war. In time, the same circle and arrow came to represent iron. Iron, of course, represents strength and security. From there, it was only a short leap to representing safety, quality, and durability.

And all those Saint Christopher medals? They've been melted down and recast into Volvo logos—if not literally, than certainly figuratively.

In taking on the role of St. Christopher, the Volvo logo summons the spirits of travel, keeping you and yours safe from harm on the highway. If it could speak, the logo would say reassuringly, "When you trust Volvo, you won't die in an accident."

Author and advertising guru Douglas Atkins suggests that the brands consumers use to define their personal identity function somewhat like religious cults. We once worshiped Saint Christopher. Now we insist on driving a Volvo.

And that Volvo, while marketed as a safe car to intelligent, granola-eating friends of the earth, has paradoxically hired Mars, the ancient god of war, to protect your family from harm.

So powerful is the Volvo brand that it was recently acquired by Geely, one of China's leading automotive manufacturers. By acquiring Volvo, Geely becomes the shepherd of Volvo's reputation for safety and reliability.

Following the announcement of the acquisition, Geely's Chairman, Li Shufu referred to the Swedish brand as *a tiger that needs to be free.* He said, "A tiger belongs to the forest, it belongs to the wild world and not confined to a zoo. We need to liberate this tiger." Chinese folklore believes that the tiger possesses divine qualities, and is dedicated to protecting people, especially children.

Invited or not, those gods will be present.

As I recall, the Marketing 101 midterm exam at the University of Pennsylvania's Wharton school in 1969 asked, "Define the term 'logo'." My nineteen-year-old self thought,

"This is one of those easy questions. Everyone knows what a logo is—that designey thing next to the brand name."

Turns out, I was wrong. As usual.

The definition of logo does begin easily. But trust me, it becomes complicated very quickly.

The root meaning of branding comes from the noun *brand*, which refers to a burning piece of wood.

American cowboys learned to mark their cattle by making distinctive scars with a piece of iron heated red-hot over a wooden fire. Such marking was called *branding,* but in the context of animal husbandry.

For example, Roy Rogers lived on the Double R Bar Ranch, whose brand (or logo) was, of course, two letter Rs side by side with a line (known as a bar in branding lingo) underneath. It looked something like this: <u>RR.</u>

A certified child of the 1950s, I remember Roy Rogers well. When I was six years old, my career ambition was to actually be Roy Rogers. I had the Roy Rogers brand hat, the Roy Rogers brand six-shooter and holster, the Roy Rogers brand lunch box, and the Roy Rogers brand plastic guitar. I did not have <u>RR</u> branded on my haunch, however.

The Roy Rogers brand stood for much more than that <u>RR</u> graphic. The Roy Rogers brand embodied archetypes such as the lone hero standing up to evil, the good husband, the sharpshooter/warrior, the musical cowboy/poet, family values, and American patriotism.

This was way before Brokeback Mountain gave a whole other meaning to the cowboy brand.

Out on the range, where Roy lived and the deer and the antelope roamed, *unbranded* cattle were considered wild and free. Take an unbranded cow into your herd, and no one cared. Rope one of those unbranded cows, and burn your Double R Bar mark onto its flank, and it became a branded cow.

Branded cattle were property.

Adding someone else's branded steer into your own herd without permission made you a cattle rustler. And cattle rustlers got hung for their crimes in the Old West. Today, you would just deal with a civil suit for trademark infringement (do you remember that country hit of 1982, *Mommas Don't Let Your Babies Grow Up To Be Intellectual Property Attorneys*? My apologies to songwriters Ed and Patsy Bruce).

The concept of the logo, or graphic identifier, is intrinsic to the entire discipline of branding.

An academic definition of the word *logo* reads, "A logo is a graphical element (ideogram, symbol, emblem, icon, sign) that, together with its logotype (a uniquely set and arranged typeface) form a trademark or commercial brand. Typically, a logo's design is for immediate recognition. The logo is one aspect of a company's commercial brand, or economic or academic entity, and its shapes, colors, fonts, and images usually are different from others in a similar market. Logos are also used to identify organizations and other non-commercial entities."

When my children were young, our home hosted two virtually identical kittens. To tell them apart, their mother and I kept the whiskers of one kitten cut short, while the other cat's whiskers grew to their full length. We had considered branding the kittens, but on second thought decided they were way too small to be roped and tied.

Those short whiskers distinguished Kitten A from Kitten B.

Mom found Kitten A much cuter than Kitten B. She began to extol the higher level of intelligence, affection, and playfulness in what became her Kitten A. Kitten B, of course, became my kitten. Kitten B was a loser.

If we had gone into the kitten business full time, our Kitten A brand logo would feature short whiskers. Our—lower price—Kitten B brand logo would feature long whiskers.

Over time, short whiskers would come to be associated with higher levels of intelligence, affection, and playfulness. Long whiskers would be seen as emblematic of doltish, unattractive, and aloof pets. Perhaps owners of long-whiskered cats would themselves come to be seen at doltish, unattractive, and aloof.

Feline analogies aside, a logo can be a simple distinguishing mark. Or it can be much more.

The word "logo" is derived from the Greek word "logos". And logos is going to take us right back to the brand gods.

Logos, pronounced low-*goes*, is an important term in philosophy, analytical psychology, rhetoric, and religion.

The ancient Greek intellectual Heraclitus (ca. 535–475 BCE) established the term *logos* in Western philosophy as meaning both the source of the cosmos, and the fundamental order of the cosmos.

We've come a long, long way from Kitten A.

This Heraclitus character was also known by several nicknames, including *The Obscure* and *The Weeping Philosopher*. Some say that Heraclitus was a loner, not to mention a wet blanket at toga parties. Given that he was prone to muttering heavy thoughts such as "you can't step twice into the same river" and "the path up and the path down are one and the same," you can see that this is a guy who could have used an image makeover. Or made a bundle writing Chinese fortune cookies.

Five hundred years after Heraclitus left his last toga party, *The Gospel of John* identified Jesus as the incarnation of the *logos*, through which all things are made. Second-century Christians identified Jesus as the *Logos* or Word of God, a distinct intermediary between God and the world. Talk about powerful brand positioning.

You'll notice that Jesus keeps turning up in this book. I wonder if Bruce Barton was actually on to something when he identified Jesus as the father of modern business.

Jesus, as logos, is represented in Christian symbolism by the eagle, which explains why a lectern shaped like an eagle stands at the front of the Holy Redeemer Episcopal Church in Bryn Mawr, PA. It is a logo.

The eagle was renowned for the power of its eye, which folklore purported could stare at the sun unharmed. The sun symbolized God's glory, and so the eagle had the power to look at God's glory full on.

You might recall that in Greek mythology Zeus, in his purest form, was also a blazing sun. One day his lover, Semele, reputed to be the mother of Dionysus, who had only experienced Zeus in his human form, asks to see him in his divine form. Zeus, unable to convince Semele that this is a bad idea, finally complies, and Semele is immediately burnt to a crisp. The eagle definitely gets a better deal with Jesus.

Brands incorporate that classic Greek concept of logos as "idea." Not just any fuzzy idea either, but the entire universe of a brand's meaning lives inside its logo. Much as the DNA inside a cell of Kitten A contains the idea of the entire cat, a logo symbolizes the entirety of a brand.

Camille Paglia, critic, historian, and political blogger, notes, "Art, no matter how minimalist, is never simply design. It is always a ritualistic reordering of reality—the modern artist who merely draws a line across a page is still trying to tame some uncontrollable aspect of reality."

Keep this in mind the next time you want to complain about the fee charged by the graphic designer you hired to create a logo for your company. She's trying to recreate the order of the universe, after all.

That quest for a ritual reordering of reality may be why so many enduring brands have mystical, or at least mysterious, figures as part of their logos. Look at the mermaid on the Starbucks logo. Most famously, study the original Proctor & Gamble logo, dating from 1851, with its depiction of the Man In the Moon and a sky with 13 stars. In 1985, P&G elected to discontinue use of that logo, after rumors flooded the country that a satanic cult was behind the consumer product giant—as if Satan really cares about clean clothes!

Over the course of the nineteenth century, manufacturers and merchants discovered the benefits of letting customers know that their particular products were better than the competition. In a classic example, uncooked oats used for oatmeal were originally sold to consumers out of big barrels, in bulk, for pennies a pound. In 1877, one of the America's larger oat processors, Henry Parsons Crowell, purchased the Quaker Mill in Ravenna, Ohio, and packed his *Quaker Oats* in a sanitary paper package with printed cooking directions.

Crowell became the first to trademark a cereal, registering those Quaker Oats in 1877. The image of a man dressed in distinctive Quaker clothing was chosen as the brand symbol because of the Quakers' reputation for honesty, integrity, hard work, and thrift. However, no Quaker ever owned the company, and the Quaker man pictured on its packages was not based on any actual individual, but was a composite of popularly perceived Quaker attributes. He was definitely a forefather of Betty Crocker!

Shoppers across the country began to ask for that oatmeal with the Quaker on the package, believing it to be of higher quality than non-branded oats sold in bulk.

Branding may begin with the application of a logo. But the power of the brand lies in the mental associations the brand conjures up in the minds of prospective purchasers and current customers. Crowell borrowed the positive attributes of Quakers to jump-start the creation of his very positive brand image.

Think of the three pointed Mercedes star. That's a logo. So is the *swoosh* on the sides of your Nike shoes. The Mercedes star symbolizes luxury, performance, and sophistication. The famous three-pointed star was designed by Gottlieb Daimler to show the ability of his motors to dominate on land, in the air, and at sea. Nike's swoosh embodies athletic performance, an enthusiastic approach to living, and an active lifestyle.

At the other end of the scale, a logo can constellate the power of the entire universe.

Just ask a devout Christian what the cross on the alter represents.

Deface the Jewish faith's six pointed Star of David logo, and you may be imprisoned for committing a hate crime.

Display a swastika, the Nazi symbol, and you can be condemned for supporting unmitigated evil.

In between the whiskers of Kitten A and the venom of the Third Reich is a vast sweep of symbolism and metaphor, where logos of all kinds signal meaning, emotion, value, and membership.

Hang the wrong color bandanna from your rear pocket, and a rival street gang will kill you. Put that Harvard "H" decal on the real window of your BMW to attract fellow wearers of the Crimson at the crew regatta. Or let the Harley-Davidson emblem on your leather jacket proclaim your rebel status to the world (even if you spend your weekdays as a PricewaterhouseCoopers accountant).

This exercise illustrates what I mean:

Go outside to your driveway. Walk up to your car. Using a pair of pliers and a screwdriver, strip off the car's nameplate from the trunk lid. Yank the logo badge off the front hood. Remove the distinguishing wheels or hubcaps.

What do you have, other than a neighbor peering fearfully at you from behind her living room curtains? No longer does your car serve as status symbol, political viewpoint signifier, or even proclaim how important the safety of your family is to you.

You now have sitting in your driveway a generic, internal combustion, personal transportation module whose sole purpose is to move you from Point A to Point B (not to be confused with Kitten A and Kitten B).

It has become a signifier without much significance.

By the way, this is an actual research technique used to determine a prospect's objective reaction to new car models. New designs are sometimes presented to research panels with all logos removed so as to get a reaction unbiased by brand perceptions. At times, a car maker will even put competitive logos on its own cars to learn how brand influences the attitudes and opinions of prospects.

Does the mere addition of a BMW logo to a Toyota increase the perceived value of the Toyota?

Yes.

While done in the name of science, I can only imagine this is great fun for the research community. And there is the germ of an idea for a killer reality show where wealthy socialites have their Gucci and Channel logos replaced with Target and Wal-Mart labels. Imagine the shame. Although at the height of the 2008 recession, some wealthy individuals were embarrassed to be seen with Tiffany and Louis Vuitton shopping bags, and did put their purchases into those Target bags.

My first father-in-law, Richard Burk, insisted that the difference between his 1975 VW Beetle and a 1975 Cadillac El Dorado was negligible, as both "had four tires and an engine." He spent most of his career as a tool and die maker. To his mechanically trained eyes, there really was great similarity in the nuts and bolts and the sheet metal that made up each car.

Biologists play that same game, insisting that Kitten A and I actually have in common about 90% of our DNA. That may be so. Nonetheless, Kitten A is a lot cuter than me.

Now, having taken off those logos from the car in your driveway, imagine if you could choose to replace them with whatever logo you wanted. What image do you want to project? What magic you want to make? What mojo will motivate your minivan?

Would you turn that Anymobile into a paradigm of luxury by anointing it with the three-pointed star of Mercedes?

Or will it be the stylized airplane propeller of the BMW, or four interlocking circles of Audi? The blue oval makes it a Ford; add the bow tie and it is a Chevrolet. Those logos, those brand names, are the animating spirits that turn the mundane into the magical.

I suspect you will not choose a Betty Crocker or a Starbucks logo to put on your car. Few of us wish to drive a box of brownies or a Frappuccino™.

However, note that Ford dresses up its Expedition SUV by offering an *Eddie Bauer* edition to emphasize that, while the Expedition is inherently rugged, there is a certain upscale cachet to that particular brand of ruggedness. According to its web site, "Eddie Bauer is an outdoor brand that offers signature outerwear; men's and women's clothing, gear and accessories; and world-class mountaineering gear."

Imagine driving a car that proclaims, "I might be parked here in the Wal-Mart lot now buying Pop-Tarts, but, after shopping, my family is going to climb Mount Whitney. In style."

Remember the Volvo logo that summoned the spirits of safe travel to keep you and yours safe on the highway?

Turns out that sometimes a logo is more than a logo.

Sometimes it is an icon.

Dr. Miriam Franco tells us "an icon is an object of the mundane world, such as an everyday material object—for example, a chalice or a goblet. However, it can become imbued with sacred meaning as it may become associated with a particular religious symbol or occurrence or represent a sacred state of being such as Sir Galahad's quest for Christ's chalice, the Holy Grail."

In other words, a simple wine glass is simply a wine glass. Until Jesus drinks from it at the Last Supper and it becomes the Holy Grail. What was a common object is now a powerful symbol, or *icon*.

"Most Western traditions of art, classical or Christian, have connected surfaces and depths in a common core of meaning; indeed the use of objects to bear symbolic meaning has been a virtually universal practice throughout human culture," notes Jackson Lears.

Doug Atkins adds, "Symbols aren't just simple one-off icons—the cross, the star, the big-bellied Buddha. They're more like a network of signs that tie together an entire set of meaning. Clothes can be symbolic, so can music, food and behaviors. Historically, these symbolic systems have been generated by cults and religions. From the first human societies onward, cults actively and consciously created distinct cultures through the orchestrated and integrated use of symbolic codes."

Those ancient religions and today's modern brand cults, says theologian Tyler Wigg Stevenson, "traffic in an economy of meaning; rendering meaningless any distinction between the sacred and the secular."

A motorcycle can be nothing more than cheap transportation in Shanghai. Build a similar bike in Milwaukee, bolt on a Harley-Davidson logo, and it becomes the signifier for a cosmos filled with rebellion, power, iconoclastic independence, patriotism, and tribal belonging.

An icon functions in a metaphoric capacity, according to Miriam Franco: "It is, on the one hand, an object with everyday meaning (the profane) and yet is transformed into a sacred object." The chalice is no longer just a goblet but a religious symbol of Christ's presence on earth (and a heck of great plot device for Monte Python) and yet, simultaneously, it is a part of one's everyday world.

The Holy Grail is both a goblet and a symbol of Christ and it later becomes synonymous with a religious quest. "But it is never anymore, just a goblet or just a symbol of Christ—a third meaning is created, just as in metaphors, and, I suspect in advertising, this is a desired state to achieve. So products are what they are and yet become imbued with other properties of the sacred world, a higher order," says Franco.

"I would think advertising would like to make a mundane object into a sacred object as well. The product is a regular object of use, or of need, but has become, via advertising, branding, and marketing, an object needed to obtain a higher state or imbued with properties beyond that of the profane world," she concludes.

An example of this transformation to a higher state is Coca Cola. Writers at The Economist magazine are fond of noting that when stripped of all brand identity, Coca-Cola is merely sweet flavored fizzy water. However, that same fizzy soda water, identified as Coca-Cola by its distinctive logo and *iconic* bottle, becomes a powerfully branded beverage. In fact, Coca-Cola is widely considered the world's strongest brand.

Viewed metaphorically, Coca Cola's brand stewards would have it represent what is best in mankind, and embody good will and fellowship among all people. Oh, and it quenches your thirst, too.

Bill Backer, creative director on the Coca-Cola account at McCann-Erickson in the 1960s, led the team that wrote one of the most powerful advertising melodies of all time. In Backer's vision, the Economist's fizzy soda water became the elixir of universal love and peace. In Coke's epic TV spot, hundreds of young adults stand on a hill singing:

> *I'd like to buy the world a home and furnish it with love,*
> *Grow apple trees and honeybees, and snow white turtledoves.*
> *I'd like to teach the world to sing in perfect harmony,*
> *I'd like to buy the world a Coke and keep it company.*
> *It's the real thing, Coke is what the world wants today.*

Is it too much to ask fizzy soda water to eliminate human conflict? No more than to see a wine goblet as the embodiment of God's power to deliver eternal salvation to the faithful.

And if a wine goblet and a glass of Coca-Cola are both icons of world peace, does that mean Jesus might be working as a soda jerk in some intergalactic—naw, probably not.

Miriam Franco might say that the outstanding production of that particular Coca-Cola television commercial transformed the Coke brand into a universal icon for peace and harmony.

Such breakthrough advertising performances are both rare and usually essential for creating brand myths where products take on something akin to holy significance.

The logo of Coca Cola and the logo of the Christian cross look very different, yet both work in parallel fashion, tapping into the human mind's wondrous ability to conjure entire universes of meaning from a single image. The study of such inner meanings is called semiotics, which we will discuss in more depth shortly.

Tyler Wigg Stevenson sees danger in the adulation of brands taken to extremes. He notes that the Bible teaches against idolatry—the worship of material objects.

"The principle behind the condemnation of idolatry; namely it represents the fallacy of giving to God's works the glory due to *God*, of ascribing transcendent qualities to non-transcendent things; of imagining that there is power in powerless objects."

"We find that we have given objects a power to create and shape us that is not naturally theirs. In a consumerist society; the fact that we are changed by the objects of our consumption—the clothes, goods, and services that make up various lifestyles—is not actually due to the objects' power. Rather, the change transpires from our shared participation in a cultural illusion."

Stevenson, writing from a decidedly Christian perspective, goes on to suggest, "…while we are certainly invested in our lifestyles, it would be a stretch to claim that as a culture we worship them. It is perhaps a bit unbelievable to say that we regard our retail-bought selves as gods; shallowness isn't idolatry."

I doubt that most of us consider that the acquisition of Nike branded merchandise, or a Harley-Davidson motorcycle, makes us into gods. But I do suggest that there is a temptation to literally idolize a Harley or the latest limited-edition celebrity-signed offering from Nike to provide that magic missing from our lives. These are minor gods, but gods nonetheless, in the sense of those *mana, spirits, and demons* referenced by Carl Jung.

All of this comes full circle when Stevenson discusses the challenge of trying to *brand* Christianity to better recruit converts:

"When it's just you and Jesus, you (the consumer) "invite him" (the product) "into your heart" (brand adoption) and "get saved" (consumer gratification). Certainly God has worked and continues to work through these formulae."

"When Christians treat the one they call Christ as a spiritual commodity, then the one they believe to be Christ is not actually the living Lord. How could he be? The Lord is not a good to be purchased or a brand to be adopted. When Christians imagine that we have Christ, what we actually have is Brand Jesus—the idol for Christianity in a consumerist age," concludes Stevenson.

I think Bruce Barton would be excited by the concept of Brand Jesus.

Tyler Wigg Stevenson writes, "Thus modern consumerism is…not a replacement of religion, but a continuation, a secularization, of a struggle for order."

Think about that. Modern consumerism is a continuation of religion and its struggle for order. That takes us back to our discussion of logo as *Logos*.

Who's that knocking at the door?

Brand Jesus or the Brand Gods?

Plato and the Archetypes

The Platonic perspective thus asks the philosopher {or the advertising copywriter} to go through the particular to the universal, and beyond the appearance to the essence.

– Richard Tarnas

In the early 1900s, the electric light bulb was regarded as a true miracle, able to bring *nature* into our homes and workplaces.

Why?

Until the advent of the electric light, there was no way to reproduce the brightness of sunlight indoors. Candles and gas lamps cast a feeble glow compared to the brilliance of a sunny day. If you needed bright light you needed daylight. Even at high noon, almost every interior room in every building on earth was darker than daylight outside.

As the miracle of electric lighting made our interiors lighter and brighter, the thought at the time was that Nature herself had been brought indoors.

Thomas Edison and his disciples proclaimed, "Let there be light."

The people saw the light, and they saw that it was good.

Sure enough, the genius of advertising was right there to spread The Word.

General Electric commissioned Maxfield Parrish, the most famous American painter and illustrator of the era, to extol the magic of its Mazda brand electric light bulbs. Note that GE named those bulbs after *Ahura Mazda*, an ancient Persian deity (yep, another brand god).

The illustrations did not show light bulbs.

Instead, paintings with evocative titles such *as Ecstasy*, *Moonlight*, and *The Lamp Seller Of Baghdad* portrayed the magic, wonder and romance of light. But they did not show light bulbs.

Perhaps Parrish recalled the words of that John Wanamaker display manager, "People do not buy the thing, they buy the effect."

A copywriter of that era, James Wallen, writing about his craft in 1925 advised, "You do not sell a man the idea of tea, but the magical spell which is brewed nowhere but in a tea-pot."

Parrish was very pleased with his illustrations, and wrote to a colleague, "I kind of wish you had seen the one [an illustration called Dreamlight] I did for the General Electric people... I think I got a little of the *spirit of the thing*. Do you know what I mean by the spirit of the thing? I mean the spirit of the things in which we take the most joy and happiness in life. The spirit of out of doors, the spirit of light and distance...that is a quality not lost on the public, I feel sure."

Parrish knew there was no magic in a picture of a light bulb. The magic lay in the powerful images and emotions that light itself could evoke. In this case, the *"the spirit of things in which we take the most joy and happiness in life. The spirit of out of doors, the spirit of light and distance..."*

Those universal images and universal ideas are known as *archetypes*. And archetypes are the hidden secret behind powerful branding.

We've seen how t-shirts adorned with Nike and Lauren and Polo and Harley-Davidson logos are really communicating the *idea* of speed, of strength, of aristocracy or wealth or sex. The magic of branding can transform a generic or commodity product into a powerful expression of the buyer's core values and essential beliefs.

Those qualities are all archetypes.

The dictionary says that archetypes are universal patterns or beliefs that are common across all peoples at all times. By employing archetypes, a brand connects with conceptual and belief patterns common to all humanity.

The word archetype is from the Greek *arkhetupon*, which literally means model, in the sense of a model being the initial version of something later multiplied. It is made up of *arkhos*, meaning chief or ruler (used also in archbishop and monarch), and *tupos*, meaning mold, model or type. Just in case you were wondering.

So if you are trying to sell something, or to create a brand, you will want to tap into those universals as part of the pitch.

Here's how it works:

The concept of *Beauty* is an archetype. While different people in different places at different times might disagree as to what particular body type, or hair color, or automobile silhouette is beautiful, they all will agree that *Beauty* is a positive attribute.

Since archetypes are ancient concepts, let's look to an ancient teacher, Plato, who helped to define archetypes as universal ideas. When I was a young man learning the craft of advertising, the name Plato never came up, except in the context of pre-AIDS Manhattan's famous sex club, *Plato's Retreat*. You can be sure there were some ancient archetypes being acted out there.

Richard Tarnas, philosopher and cultural historian, has written extensively on archetypes, "Plato taught that what is perceived as a particular object in the world can be understood as a concrete expression of a more fundamental Idea, *an archetype* which gives that object its special structure and condition."

Tarnas continues, "A particular thing is what it is by virtue of the Idea informing it. Something is beautiful to the exact extent that the archetype of Beauty is present in it. When one falls in love, it is *Beauty* that one recognizes and surrenders to, the beloved object being Beauty's instrument or vessel. The essential factor in the event is the archetype, and it is this level that carries the deepest meaning."

Something is beautiful because the archetype of beauty is present. An ugly horse does not have Beauty within. The spirit, the archetype, of Beauty, inhabits a beautiful horse.

"The essential factor in the event is the archetype," continues Tarnas, " and it is this level that carries deeper meaning."

Archetype can be a generic version of a personality. Jung repeatedly refers to personality types commonly found in fiction as archetypes—the *hero* being the one most frequently used. But to Jung they are far more than recognizable characters—in fact, they are not at all characters, but symbolic gateways to truths about human condition and to the path of personal enlightenment.

Archetypes reveal the workings of the world, serving as learning tools providing lessons from primordial time about what leads mankind to great accomplishments—and to abject tragic failure.

View any of Monet's *Water Lilies* paintings, and you might feel a sense of wonder, experience an elevation of the spirit, or fall into a dreamy trance imagining your soul wandering amid the lilies. That is the archetype of Beauty at work. Imagine if you can evoke similar feelings in a prospective buyer of your product.

Dr. Miriam Franco of Immaculata University tells us "images that are the most transformative for people tend to be ones that evoke sensory perception. You take them in not as thoughts or statements but as something that is felt, seen, heard, tasted in the body and connected as well to timeless, universal human symbols that represent basic human needs and experiences." In other words, archetypal images carry the most power.

Franco continues, "when conducting guided imagery workshops, if I invite people to imagine their ideal place of relaxation—for majority of Americans, it is the beach. But it is not necessarily the most exotic beach or the ultimate beach. It is a strip of sand, the water meeting the horizon (even if it is not the purest blue), the sound of the waves lapping against the shoreline, or hearing the sea gulls chirping or smelling the salt moisty air. It can be the beach at Hoboken; it does not matter, *it is the beach*."

"The beach always symbolizes nature, it symbolizes (on the coast) an everyday part of one's geography. In fact, most major cities in the US on the east or west coast are harbors. So even in the most mundane urban cities whose harbors do not have the most sacred looking of shorelines, the beach becomes sacred."

People respond to the archetype of beach. The specific example of any beach is a portal leading to the universal qualities of that archetypal beach where peace, relaxation, and refreshment of spirit prevail.

This is because the archetype itself is part of the immortal timeless fabric of the universe. *Beauty* and the *beach* have existed forever, and will exist forevermore, with or without human intervention.

"The Platonic perspective thus asks the philosopher [or the advertising copywriter] to go through the particular to the *universal*, and beyond the appearance to the *essence*. It assumes not only that such insight is possible, but that it is mandatory for the attainment of true knowledge," says Tarnas.

"Plato directs the philosopher's attention away from the external and concrete, from taking things at face value, and points deeper and inward so that the objects one perceives with one's senses are actually crystallizations of more primary essences, which can be apprehended only by the active, intuitive mind."

At the risk of being too literal, the classic DeBeers' copy line, *A Diamond Is Forever*, taps into this archetypal power. The beauty of a diamond is forever, because *Beauty* is forever. And the diamond becomes an icon (see previous chapter), which captures the essence of eternal beauty.

DeBeers brands diamonds for engagement rings by associating this idea of forever with the archetype of love. As I slip the engagement ring, with its perfect diamond, onto the finger of my betrothed, the diamond says, "Our love, like this diamond, is forever."

Our love becomes eternal. Our love exists beyond time and space, where those archetypes—which provide the foundation of the universe—exist. We become immortal, and at one with the universe, as I give you this diamond. And to be at one with the universe is to be at one with God. Thus our love becomes a manifestation of the divine.

Not a bad trick for a sparkly piece of rock and a clever N.W. Ayer Advertising Agency copywriter named Frances Gerety. As Gerety remembers it, "Dog tired, I put my head down and said, 'Please God, send me a line'." Then she wrote, *A Diamond is Forever*. Was that the answer of a Brand God?

Carl Jung said, "Archetypes create myths, religions, and philosophical ideas that influence and set their stamp on whole nations and epochs."

Joseph Campbell elaborated on the connection between archetypes and the universal themes found in myths common across all societies and cultures.

"These bits of information from ancient times, which have to do with the themes that have supported human life, built civilizations, and informed religions over the millennia, have to do with deep inner problems, inner mysteries, inner thresholds of passage, and if you don't know what the guide-signs are along the way, you have to work it our yourself. But once this subject catches you, there is such a feeling, from one or another of these traditions, of information of a deep, rich, live-vivifying sort that you don't want to give it up."

Very often, advertising retells these ancient myths, triggering desire and longing deep inside the consumer's psyche.

The Maxfield Parrish example demonstrates Plato's teaching that the philosopher's attention must be directed away from the external and concrete, from taking things at face value, and pointing deeper and inward so that the objects one perceives with one's senses are actually crystallizations of more primary essences, which can be apprehended only by the active, intuitive mind.

Richard Tarnas notes, "Platonic ideas [archetypes] are objective. They do not depend on human thought, but exist entirely in their own right. They are perfect patterns, embedded in the very nature of things. The Platonic Idea is not merely a human idea, but the *universe's idea*, an ideal entity that can express itself externally in concrete tangible form or internally as a concept in the human mind. It is a primordial image or formal essence that can manifest in various ways and on various levels, and is the foundation of reality itself."

The idea of a Mercedes automobile as a beautiful object becomes the expression of a universal concept, which can exist outside of man's particular knowledge.

And, taken to its most refined level, these archetypal concepts help to create reality itself.

With cup holders and leather seats, no less.

The Significance of Signifiers

There is nothing doggy about the word dog.

– Catherine Belsey

One other abstract concept plays an essential role in creating brands. This one is called *semiotics*.

To begin the lesson, relax in a comfortable easy chair. Take a few deep breaths. Light a stick of incense if you wish.

Then listen as I say in a pleasant, soothing voice, "Use your imagination to think about ancient Egypt, and the Mesopotamians in the cradle of civilization with their fertile crescent."

What comes to mind when you think of those ancient civilizations?

Miss Pavelka comes immediately to my mind whenever I hear the word Mesopotamia. She was my fifth grade teacher at the Chatham Township, New Jersey elementary school. Miss Pavelka tried – with little success – to convince a skeptical crowd of ten year olds that Hammurabi was of any interest whatsoever.

Clearly, Ancient Mesopotamia could use better branding.

Which showed up when Steve Martin rhymed *Babylonia* with *Condo made of stone-i-ah* in his 1979 musical ode to King Tut. Finally, I was able to form a positive association with things Mesopotamian. Unfortunately, Miss Pavelka was by then long retired from teaching, convinced she had failed to reach my inner archeologist.

At the mention of ancient Egypt today, my mind fills with thoughts of pyramids, Isis, scarabs, sand, the Nile, Cleopatra, King Tut, and riding a yellow school bus to the Metropolitan Museum of Art to view mummies and hieroglyphics.

Walking from the bus towards the museum, paired off with a field trip partner, I got to hold hands with my secret fifth grade crush, Martha Schwerin—whose image now also appears every time I see a picture of a sphinx.

My wandering mind begins to wonder how the pyramids were constructed using only simple hand tools, stone ramps, and Moses. My heart begins to race when I recall those mummy movies where the undead dead have to be killed again.

That torrent of images and emotions (along with memories of Martha Schwerin) provoked by the idea of Egypt in my subconscious mind are the essence of branding.

Contrary to what your advertising agency might tell you, branding is not all about dancing polar bears and Super bowl ads with catchy jingles and celebrity endorsements.

The power of branding lies in the impressions, values, attributes, memories, and desires that involuntarily flood out of your subconscious at the mention of a particular brand.

You are the one who determines what that bottle of Coke means. Your personal life experiences—not some clever woman on Madison Avenue—define the Coke brand that lives in your head. Brands are not contained in logos or slogans or strategy documents. They live inside of our brains. And, for a lucky few brands, they live in our hearts as well.

Of course, the Coca-Cola Company will spend hundreds of millions of dollars on dancing polar bears and Simpsons-themed TV commercials trying to plant thoughts favorable to Coke in your mind.

That's called brand building. And sometimes it works as planned by all those high priced marketing strategists, social media mavens, and creative directors.

My own pleasant childhood memories of gingham table cloths and sharing Coca-Cola on family picnics are counter-pointed by the 1981 memory of the world's worst hangover following a misguided night of native rum mixed with warm Coca-Cola on a mid-winter St. Thomas vacation. That particular hangover ranks among the top reasons I finally quit drinking alcohol.

Deep in my twisted mind live two opposite thoughts:

Thought # 1—Coca Cola means love and family
Thought # 2—Coca Cola and rum will melt my brain

This may not be what Coke's marketing team in Atlanta intended, but that's the challenge of marketing. No matter how hard the branding gurus try, your impressions of the brand will be formed by your personal experience, Super Bowl advertisements of dancing polar bears notwithstanding.

I still drink Coke and, sometimes, inexplicably hallucinate apple trees, honeybees, and snow-white turtledoves.

The fancy word embracing all of this imagery and symbolism is *semiotics*. Semiotics is one of those words used by linguists and PhDs much more frequently than by copywriters and account executives.

Nonetheless, semiotics lies at the heart of branding and brand making.

Semiotics is the study of *how symbols communicate meaning*.

Those symbols can be signs, words, logos, or even gestures such as raising a middle finger, or arching an eyebrow.

What we call a symbol is a term, a name, or even a picture that may be familiar in daily life, yet that possesses specific connotations in addition to its conventional and obvious meaning. We constantly use symbolic terms to represent concepts we cannot define completely, or fully comprehend. This is one reason why all religions employ symbolic language or images.

Those signs or symbols consist of two elements. One element is the *signifier*, which is the actual sign or symbol itself. The other element, which has virtually infinite dimension, is the signified—the information which the symbol seeks to communicate.

Our language is comprised of symbols. In English, *dog* is the symbol for that four legged barking creature that has fleas. In French, *chien* is its symbol. In Russian, Lassie is a *sobaka*. The symbol changes; what is signified, that *dog,* remains constant.

Catherine Belsey, in her book *Poststructuralism,* says, "...on the one hand, the *signifier,* the sound or the visual appearance of the word, phrase, or image in question; on the other, the signified, its meaning. In ordinary circumstances, the distinction is purely methodological: we rarely see a signifier which does not signify, or mean something."

This is true so long as you speak the language, or know the signaling system. Imagine, though, that you find yourself in a foreign country, and do not know the language at all. Belsey continues, "An unknown language consists entirely of signifiers in isolation. We hear sounds and assume that they signify, since we see native speakers apparently communicating, but to us they mean nothing... the relationship between the signifier and the signified is arbitrary. There is nothing *doggy* about the word dog."

"Neither element of the sign determines the other: the signifier does not 'express' the meaning, nor does the signified 'resemble' the form or sound...Isolated visual signifiers are familiar to us, after all, in the form of road signs or brand logos."

When the first space alien lands on earth and sees a Coca Cola logo, I suspect she will not think about frosty cold drinks at summer picnics.

Branding consultant Grant Venner, on his UK-based web site *Brand Semiotics Limited* suggests, "Semiotics is like a magic pair of glasses that allows you to see through to the heart of things. The more you look, the more you want to know."

Venner proposes that brands have a hard side; characterized by the facts and figures of the product, mission statements, and brand descriptions.

But, he continues, brands have a soft side, comprised of "all the connections a brand has ever made with its consumers. In so doing, it takes its place within, and resonates against, a culture or cultures. These connections are deeper, and consumers generally can't articulate them…Brands make connections with culture in complex yet subtle ways; they can both resonate powerfully against culture, and fall out of step with culture."

I was the Marketing Director for Playboy Magazine in 1985-86. Playboy was a brand that resonated against—and with—its culture. A 1964 trade advertisement read:

"What Sort Of Man Reads Playboy?

A young man who knows his way around—uptown or downtown—the PLAYBOY reader's arrival signals the start of an eventful evening. And with good taste—from wine to women…"

In the 1950s, Playboy was viewed as pornographic and even dangerous.

By the early 1960s, Playboy was cool and sophisticated in the manner of James Bond. I remember when my father joined the Playboy Club in 1962. He was a marketing manager for Listerine mouthwash, and Listerine advertised in Playboy—as part of the deal, he received a free membership at its club. My mother readily accompanied him in his white 1961 Oldsmobile 98 on nighttime visits to the Manhattan home of the Playboy Bunny on East 59th Street. Dinner, drinks, and dancing at the Playboy Club conferred an image of urban sophistication on both my staid father and my most conventional mother, who enjoyed the frisson of naughtiness conferred by Playboy.

After the hippies and their sexual revolution, Playboy struggled to define what made it culturally relevant. During my tenure, Playboy was besieged on the right by fundamentalist Christians who condemned us for destroying family values. On the left, Esquire, Rolling Stone, and Details magazine were redefining male hipness and male style. Playboy had become neither hip, nor smart, or daring.

Today, in a world overflowing with no-cost online pornography, Playboy persists as a parody of itself and has come close to bankruptcy. Who needs to pay for Playboy's PG-rated pictures of naked women when XXX material helps finance the entire internet? The sophistication and intelligence (think of Dave Brubeck) which once informed the Playboy brand has been replaced by the reality show version of Viagra-fueled octogenarian Hugh Hefner in pajama-clad romps, accessorized by matching blondes who could be his grandchildren.

When the Playboy rabbit head, drenched in artificial pine tree scent, was reduced to dangling from the rear view mirror of a rattling Checker cab on New York's Tenth Avenue, we lost our belief. The magic was gone. The brand had come to represent men who were clueless regarding women. In Venner's words, Playboy now resonated powerfully against culture.

The Playboy tag line continues to read *Entertainment for Men.* Increasingly, however, the men are not entertained.

As Playboy failed to recapture its stature as a knowing voice defining American male sexuality and coolness, the signifier came to symbolize brand failure.

Confessions of a Mad Man

The best minds of a generation were stirred to fabricate illusions.

— Randal Rothenberg

If the Brands are gods, and Consumerism our common religion, whom are the practitioners creating, shaping, and sustaining this vast faith?

In the ancient and indigenous worlds, priests, priestesses, shamans, wizards, and witches knew how to attract the favor of the gods. They told those seeking to please the gods:

"Eat this, and be cured."

"Drink this, and become a Man."

"Wear this, and be safe from all enemies."

"Drive this, and seduce all you meet."

Actually, "Drive this" is not an ancient command but a preview of how modern marketers have assumed the role of shaman as the ancient gods take up residence inside contemporary brands.

Today's pantheon of Brand Gods are attended to by its own priests and priestesses who take the guise of brand managers,

copywriters, marketing planners, public relations practitioners, social media managers, art directors, and, of course, the
crew of the Good Year blimp.

On occasion, I myself have been a Brand God acolyte labor-
ing on Madison Avenue and its many tributaries. After writing
this book, I'll probably be excommunicated from marketing
communications. With that, I will become an expert on marketing excommunications.

Edward Bernays, the father of public relations, believed
there were only a handful of professionals who truly understood
"the mental processes of the masses."

Bernays was convinced that the thinking of the public at
large was subject to manipulation by those few who understood
the secret to influencing behavior. Believing that the public's
judgment was "not to be relied upon," he feared that "they
could very easily vote for the wrong man or want the wrong
thing, so that they had to be guided from above." These few
masters of persuasion had outsized influence on politics and
business.

Long before the term "viral marketing" was every used,
Bernays understood the power of influential early adapters for
shaping public perception across an entire society.

Should we be surprised that Bernays was a nephew of
Sigmund Freud, who was so interested in the power of sugges-
tion to influence behavior?

Bernays, whose career began in 1913, sought to transform
the advertising practitioner from a lineal descendant of the

circus advance man into a respected professional. He emphasized the limits of human malleability, along with the importance of playing on existing beliefs and prejudices. He advocated the application of psychology and group dynamics, using a scientific approach to shaping public opinion described as the engineering of consent.

Echoing Miriam Franco, William Leach comments, "Bernays was a shrewd promoter who know how to transform the profane into an imitation of the sacred..."

Author Jackson Lears describes how public opinion acquired transcendent qualities, "The ideal of public opinion was rooted in the managerial professionals' need to locate a transcendent source of meaning, a secure basis for values, in a society whose religious and moral foundations were increasingly problematic." The people had an almost magical ability to "make it so" just by force of opinion.

Randall Rothenberg touches on marketing's power to transform the profane into, at the very least, an imitation of the sacred. He describes how Subaru of America, seeking to create a new brand image, reviewed six advertising agencies and finally awarded its account to Weiden & Kennedy.

Then, after a year of Herculean effort, Weiden & Kennedy fails, and is fired.

A successor agency is hired and, managed by a sadder but wiser client, success comes to Subaru at last.

The final paragraphs of Rothenberg's book notes, "Subaru of America had learned the lesson of advertising—as the great ad man Bruce Barton had acknowledged decades before, advertising was 'something big, something splendid—something which goes deep down into an institution and gets hold of the soul of it.'"

The advertising practitioner is engaged in corporate soul tending.

Millennia before advertising copywriters or market researchers walked the land, indigenous cultures believed that each tree, rock, stream, bird, and insect carried its own animating spirit.

Such spirits were revered, and often propitiated with offerings from those who were grateful for the bounty they provided. You can see this in action in the film *Avatar*, when the blue skinned Na'vi hunters thank their prey for giving their lives to nourish the tribe.

Today, I'm unaware of anyone who prays to *Snap*, or *Crackle*, or *Pop* before pouring milk on their morning Rice Krispies.

But should they?

As noted earlier, legions of advertising account executives, market researchers, art directors, tweeters, and those blimp pilots, are at work around the globe trying to persuade you that their particular brand of beer or athletic shoe or cold cereal holds the key to your life's success, health, and happiness.

Some textbooks refer to these people as brand missionaries, conjuring visions of nineteenth century Methodists in pith helmets steaming up the Congo River in search of heathens to convert.

We have seen in the writings of Calkins and Bernbach that the most passionate advertising practitioners can believe that their work has a sacred dimension.

While at *Playboy*, my job involved helping the advertising sales staff compete against the likes of *Sports Illustrated* and *Penthouse* for advertising schedules. I wrote presentations, helped to create audience research, and plotted selling strategies.

Most advertisers had no difficulty putting their advertising messages next to pictures of naked woman. After all, they were trying to sell to *men.*

Some advertisers had guidelines that prohibited advertising in publications that were *pornographic.* This was a time of renewed evangelical fervor in the heartland, with the Reverend Donald Wildmon's *National Federation for Decency* demanding boycotts of advertisers who invested in *Penthouse, Hustler*, and other adult magazines he believed were destroying America's family values—including Hugh Hefner's family business, *Playboy*.

I remember several meetings with Christie Hefner where she became quite the scholar, describing why the naked women featured in *Playboy* were *not* pornographic, while the naked women featured in *Penthouse* were, in fact, clearly obscene.

Hour after hour was spent in conference rooms full of *Playboy* advertising sales professionals, both men and women who, with Talmudic intensity, would pore over the subtleties of pose and degree of revelation between *Playboy's* naked women, and those found in the evil *Penthouse* magazine. We sought to prove that *Playboy* was art; *Penthouse* was porn.

I was very dedicated to my work. After all, this was a holy calling. And I was part of the family.

Try as we might, my advertising sales colleagues at *Playboy* were never able to come up with an objective way to separate the pornographic nude photos from those that were merely artistic celebrations of the female form and the joy of heterosexuality.

As a young Mad Man, I was trained to believe the market is rational, because we live in a world that demands objective, scientific proof of that which is factual and real. I cannot make a claim that my client's brand of snow tire has more stopping power on ice than any other tire, unless I back it up with expensive third party research that the Federal Trade Commission recognizes as being fair and balanced. Snow tires are one sort of reality. Naked women are much less subject to objective classification.

I used to tell my clients that there is a scientific, psychologically sound, and totally logical method for building brands. I was wrong.

Considering that 90% of new products fail after their introduction, you can see that brand building mimics the spawning of salmon. Stick with me on this one.

The female salmon can lay 10,000 eggs in one season. But only a very few, perhaps five or ten, of those eggs grow to maturity and return to the river of their birth to spawn again.

Brands behave much the same way. Of thousands and thousands of new products launched in any given year, very few return to spawn in the river of their birth.

Those failures come in spite of tremendous investment in market research intended to better understand customer likes, dislikes, motivations, needs and wants. Total 2010 advertising spending was $131 billion. How much of it was wasted?

Marketers are optimists by nature, believing that every brand contains at least a fragment of the DNA that caused Coke and Nike and Starbucks to become global icons.

Today we can genetically engineer strawberries to taste like pineapples, and create tomatoes that stay fresh for weeks. We can clone sheep, and dogs, and kittens, and even salmon.

But we can't clone Nike, and there is no magic marketing gene that can transform dud products into superbrands. You can petition the Brand Gods with prayer, but they may answer you with an Edsel.

William Goldman, a Hollywood veteran who wrote the script for *Butch Cassidy and the Sundance Kid,* is renowned for noting that, when it comes to making movies, "Nobody knows anything."

Goldman was observing that no one could reliably predict or prescribe what made a hit movie. If they could, there would be no flops.

Why is it that the best producer and the best director and the best actors and great music and great cinematography can create a great flop? And occasionally the film by a first time writer with a first time director with a miniscule six-figure budget walks off with the Oscar and tops the box office?

Nobody knows anything.

Just as ancient and indigenous tribes sacrifice the chief who fails, the ad agency gets fired periodically so as to bring in fresh energy to the marketing effort. In my early advertising days, I learned that, the day you celebrate signing a new account, you are also one day closer to being fired for losing that account.

Of course, miracles do happen.

Coca-Cola began life as a patent medicine (remember them?) called *Pemberton's French Wine Coca*. It was sold as a nerve tonic, stimulant, and headache remedy. When a local prohibition law in Atlanta required that the alcohol be removed, pharmacist John Pemberton reformulated his tonic to include sugar rather than alcohol. No billion dollar-branding genius was consulted.

The Nike swoosh was quickly scribbled after an impatient printer asked what to put on the shoeboxes for an early ship-ment of sneakers. Neither Steve Jobs nor Bill Bernbach or Andy Warhol contributed their genius—only some part time graphic designer named Carolyn Davidson, student at Portland State University. Her fee, incidentally, was $35.00, a pretty good price for reordering the universe, per Camille Paglia.

The Starbucks mermaid was R-rated in her original bare-breasted incarnation, attempting to be faithful to the nautical heritage of the original Starbuck, who served as first mate in of Melville's novel, Moby *Dick*.

In the beginning, on the first page of Brand Genesis, neither Coke nor Nike nor Starbucks had any sense of their ultimate destiny. This is why I suggest that most books about branding are misguided. No one really knows for certain how to create a powerful, world changing, epochal brand—notwithstanding what *The Economist* teaches us.

You see that principle at work when a company called *Amazon* becomes the world's biggest online bookseller. Are there any branding consultants who would have recommended "Amazon" as the name for a pioneering Internet bookseller?

What does *eBay* have to do with auctions?

Why would I buy a $3,000 leather sofa from a store called *Restoration Hardware?*

Wise advertisers and brand managers heed the legendary economist Maynard Keynes who reminds us that the vitality of the marketplace is due as much to animal spirits as to rational thinking.

The father of modern economics, Adam Smith, referred to these forces as the invisible hand of the market.

Business historian Jackson Lears suggests that the unpredictable, seemingly irrational, process of creating advertising hints at the "possibility of mystery in the cosmos, a hint of animistic alternatives to the dualism of the dominant culture."

> Animal Spirits.
> Invisible Hands.
> Mystery in the Cosmos.

None of those were part of the undergraduate Introduction To Marketing course I took at the Wharton School. Strangely, they were part of that Anthropology 101 course.

Jackson Lears writes of a 1923 J. Walter Thompson new business presentation wherein the agency said, "You can write as emotionally about ham as about Christianity." We believe in our power to bring at least temporary transcendence to bottled soda, or canned ham.

"The words agencies use to describe the process [of creating advertising]," says Randall Rothenberg, "seem culled from anthropology. Accounts are pursued like animals in the hunt; the executives charged with finding accounts through the interpretation of street gossip are rain makers; headhunters are retained to locate the marketing or creative experts who can be dragged in, at a price, to help the pursuit."

You know those anthropologists. Always looking for gods and demons and spirits.

Movie buffs will remember the 1948 Cary Grant / Myrna Loy film, *Mr. Blandings Builds His Dream House.* Cary Grant plays the role of an advertising executive about to lose his job because he cannot think of a powerful slogan to promote the *Wham* brand of ham.

In the film's climatic scene, Grant is resigned to failure, when his family cook, Gussie, played by Louise Beavers, announces that dinner is served. She proudly notes that she is serving *Wham* brand ham, because, "If you ain't eating *Wham*, you ain't eating ham!" Gussie was channeling the Brand Gods.

The day is saved, and Mr. Blandings is able to afford that dream house after all.

Thomas Moore describes how, in the sixteenth century, Paracelus advised physicians, "The physician should speak of that which is invisible. What is visible should belong to his knowledge, and he should recognize illnesses, just as anyone who is not a physician can recognize them from their symptoms. But this is far from making him a physician; he becomes a physician only when he knows that which is unnamed, invisible and immaterial, yet has its effect."

In the spirit of Paracelus, I now I tell my clients, "We can craft the perfect strategy, bring forth advertising copy whose brilliance puts Shakespeare to shame, support it all with Facebook and Twitter and product placement and expensive global media efforts to put your logo in front of every man, woman, and child from Boston to Beijing. But without a bit of luck, a bit of good fortune, a touch of divine providence, the whole thing might still crash and burn."

Product failures tend to sink beneath the waves into unmarked graves, like the Atari computer, or that Edsel, or Pets.com or Kellogg's Cereal Mate—cereal plus milk in one package!

Branding is a mystery—now deepened as social media and digital marketing take branding viral. For centuries, marketers controlled the media that carried their messages. Suddenly customers *are* the media, transmitting the news—good and bad—about the brands they use, the goods they buy, the stores they shop. How do I tell my clients that I know how to make their YouTube video explode with 20 million views overnight?

Certainly we marketers have our share of successes. Snapples and Apples do happen every year.

This has nothing to do with a lack of talent or intelligence on the part of those who create brands and make advertising. We are a bright group of likable men and women.

Finbar Taggit, the pseudo-anonymous British hedge fund blogger, says that his branding people are "way smarter than any of us but suffer from lack of cohesion and drive to make money." This has been my personal experience. Just look at that $35.00 Nike logo. Advertising practitioners, myself included, fancy themselves as the smartest people in the room. We are seldom the wealthiest people in the room.

Randall Rothenberg, observing the modern advertising business, wrote, "The best minds of a generation were stirred to fabricate illusions."

"As the [twentieth] century drew to its close, young men and women were increasingly using their creative powers not to convey high truths or poetry but to dream up five-word slogans. The experts were saying that products and services were now so much alike, in category after category, that the only element that could distinguish one company's products from another's was image [brand]. Wall Street said that a strong brand could actually add value to a firm's yield."

Why else would someone charge with VISA rather than MasterCard, lather with Ivory instead of Dial, or drive a Volvo rather a Camry?

If the poet Homer was the voice of ancient Greece, Paglia says, "I recognized commercial popular culture as the authentic native voice of America."

Way back in 1912, the trade magazine *Judicious Advertising* reported, "To create good selling copy advertisement writers must be bubbling over with enthusiasm. A day's work with the glow of magic fire is worth a week of galley slave plugging."

Jackson Lears notes, "Since the late nineteenth century, advertising has given people who like to write, draw, or shoot film the opportunity to get paid regularly (maybe even well) for it."

No matter how warmly that magic fire may glow, the life of a Mad Man (or Woman) is not without sacrifice. At the dawn of the modern marketing era, Theodore Dreiser created a character named Eugene Wirtla for his novel *The Genius (1915),* whose rise in the advertising corporate hierarchy "requires him to abandon his romantic dream of autonomous creativity to embrace a new career in impression management."

Sometimes, those engaged in impression management have doubts about the value of their craft.

Jackson Lears, reviewing the state of the advertising business in the first decades of the twentieth century observed, "Advertising executives and copywriters stood in a problematic relationship to the emerging discourse of mass society. They claimed to be among the relatively small number of persons who understood the mental processes of the masses, but they were not always clear about whether they were serving the sovereign consumer or channeling her desires."

For a few years in the 1970s, I was an account executive at the giant McCann-Erickson advertising agency in Manhattan. Working to help sell copies of the New York Times, I was privileged to be teamed with some of McCann's top talent. These few men and women carried the torch for several of America's leading brands.

At that time, McCann was handing advertising for Coca-Cola. Creative director Bill Backer had authored the legendary I'd *Like To Buy The World A Coke* jingle and oversaw its block-buster TV commercial with hundreds of happy young people singing on a hillside.

If you are old enough, you still remember the Mean Joe Greene TV spot for Coke, where a terrifyingly fierce football linebacker gives the shirt off his back to a young boy who hands him a refreshing bottle of Coke after a tough game. Copywriter Penny Hawkey and art director Roger Mosconi were responsible for that one.

A senior art director named Bob Lenz was playing a pivotal role filming the pioneering *Tastes Great/Less Filling* spots for *Miller Lite* beer.

I was present at a creative meeting where the latest advertising campaign to promote readership of the New York Times was being conceived. Leading the meeting was Bob Lenz, that art director of Miller Lite fame.

As a group, we struggled to find yet another way to persuade the public to read what we knew was the world's greatest newspaper.

A silence had descended on the room as the flow of ideas slowed, and then stopped completely.

You could hear a clock ticking—or the dripping of nervous perspiration from my worried brow. How do I tell my client, *The New York Times*, that we were out of ideas?

Randall Rothenberg says, "Creative people are the high priests who invoke God's inspiration."

At that moment, we were all looking for a bit of inspiration, holy or otherwise, to sell more newspapers.

Suddenly Bob Lenz sat bolt upright at the conference table, grabbed for a drawing pad and black marker, literally shouting, "I've got it!" Filled with hope and relief, we watched as he furiously scribbled the idea that we knew was going to save the account and make us all heroes.

"There it is," he beamed, holding aloft his genius inspiration for all to see.

In bold script he had written, *SAY HELLO TO A GOOD BUY.*

Invited or not, sometimes the gods simply refuse to show up.

End Note: A Personal Story

We're not those kind of people.

— Walter Pershing Kuenstler

Walter Pershing Kuenstler, my dad, graduated with a marketing degree in 1940 from the Wharton School at the University of Pennsylvania. He rose to the rank of Captain during World War II in the Army Air Forces, ultimately flying B-17 bombers into Germany as Hitler made his last stand in a Berlin bunker during May of 1945.

Four years to the month later, I was born in Englewood, NJ, in the shadow of the George Washington Bridge. My mother was Ruby Julia Grant, a daughter of Montgomery, Alabama who met my aviation cadet father while he was stationed at nearby Maxwell Field.

By the time I entered third grade, my dad was a marketing research manager for General Foods in White Plains, N.Y. General Foods, now absorbed into giant Kraft Foods, was the preeminent manufacturer and seller of packaged foods. The General Foods brand portfolio included Post cereals, Maxwell House Coffee, Jell-O, Log Cabin Syrup, Kool-Aid, and Birds Eye.

Birds Eye, the first line of frozen foods ever, had been acquired by General Foods, and was a special favorite of my dad, who marveled how vegetables and fruits (such as strawberries, which were only available during a limited growing season when he was a boy) were now sold year round, on-demand, in easy-to-prepare frozen form. He was proud to be part of this progress.

My older sister Marcy and I were involuntarily recruited to taste-test various General Foods products still in early development, before actual test marketing with real consumers began. Today we call this the beta testing stage.

I have vivid childhood memories of my father coming home from work one night with a brown cardboard box containing a dozen clear glass jars filled with orange powder. The powder had the consistency of granulated sugar—which actually was its major component.

The jars resembled peanut butter jars. Each had a plain white label reading *Sample A, Sample B, Sample C* and so forth. The word *CONFIDENTIAL* was stamped ominously onto each label.

The next morning at breakfast, with a concentration befitting the Japanese tea ceremony, Dad sat Marcy and me at the kitchen table. Measuring carefully, my mother mixed the powder from each jar into separate glass tumblers of cold water for each of us.

With a precision from his days as a military pilot, Dad instructed us to sip from each glass, just once.

"Was it too sweet? Too tart? Did you like it?" he asked for each of the twelve samples. The answers were carefully recorded in his neat script on a preprinted General Foods Research Department form, with carbon paper duplicate.

The powder was colored pale orange. Mixed into cold water, the resulting beverage had a distinct, if artificial, orange flavor. Some samples tasted very sweet, like orange popsicles; others were so tart as to hurt my tongue. One or two of the samples actually tasted ok.

No one told my sister and me that the somewhat tangy beverage also contained a full day's worth of Vitamin C.

Six months later, Dad brought home another cardboard box containing the fruits of his research. It was an early production case of *Tang®*, the "needs no refrigeration, store right in your kitchen pantry" instant breakfast drink. Food historians note that *Tang* officially went on sale in 1959.

In 1965, the Gemini astronauts took *Tang* into orbit and minor immortality. I suppose, in my tiny way, that was my contribution to the conquest of outer space.

My mother always kept a jar of *Tang* in the cupboard, just in case the world's supply of orange juice ran out.

A brilliant General Foods chemist, Dr. William A. Mitchell, invented Tang. Mitchell was also responsible for *Pop Rocks* candy, and that staple of the World War II soldier, powdered eggs. Once upon a time, chefs created new foods. Now we have food chemists.

The May 1959 issue of General Food's in-house employee magazine explained that among the obstacles faced by scientists at General Foods were getting stable, water-soluble forms of vitamin C into the powder, finding just the right semi-opaque orange additive, and finding a way to keep the powder from caking in the jar. When it came time to package Tang, marketing people (including my father) took an unusual step (for 1959) and created a label that actually informed consumers of the nutritional value they would get in every glassful of Tang. That dose of Vitamin C had become a Unique Selling Proposition.

There were other products from Dr. Mitchell's laboratory to be tested, including a line of dehydrated gourmet dinners (all starch and no flavor) that mercifully never made it to market, and a cereal shaped like the letters of the alphabet that I truly disliked. Notwithstanding my distaste, *Alpha-Bits*® did go on to become a top seller for the General Foods Post Cereals division.

The sons of Cherokee Indians were taught by their fathers to look for the spoor of deer, to learn what plants made good medicine, and to forecast the weather from the color of leaves blowing in the wind.

Dad would take me to the neighborhood A&P grocery store to study how the jars of Tang were displayed on its shelves. Those in the marketing profession call this activity a store check. Store checks are intended to see how retailers are merchandising your products, and to observe what your competition may be doing to steal customers away from you.

My father taught me to look for end-aisle displays, to count the number of product facings for competitive products, and to see if the signs that read *Tang on Sale* were properly placed on the shelves.

Under his expert marketing tutelage, I learned how to spot subtle changes in a competitor's packaging, to notice how Birds Eye streamlined its logo to read better on TV, to observe that Rice Krispies now came in single serving boxes, and that sometimes a *two for one* sale was no sale at all!

He was the wise marketing chief, I his faithful companion and pupil, ever fascinated by his stories about how changing the color on a package could increase sales, why shelf position mattered, and where to put in-store signage for greatest effect. You'll notice that best selling items are usually at eye level, as are featured items on sale. Slow moving commodities like white flour, sugar, and tomato sauce are usually on the lowest shelf.

American Indians named their children after a characteristic behavior, such as *Running Deer* or *Sleeps with Wolves*. I suppose my Cherokee name would have been *Brand Boy*.

Automobiles were responsible for one of my seminal lessons in branding—and sociology. I was five years old, and had been watching the *Disneyland* show on television with my parents and sister.

The show ended with a sixty second commercial for the long-defunct Rambler automobile. The Rambler was a low-priced compact car produced by American Motors. The commercial promised performance, style, and togetherness for the family that drove a Rambler.

I turned and asked my father, "Why don't we buy a Rambler?"

Giving me a stern look, he said, "Because we are not *that* sort of people."

Oops.

In an instant, I learned another way of looking at the world. I discovered that *my* kind of people did not own Ramblers. The look on my dad's face signaled that there was something to be disliked about people who did own Ramblers. It was *us* versus the *Rambler owners*. They were not of our tribe.

Memories of those Rambler owners resurfaced when my wife and I created Kitten A and Kitten B. From a semiotic perspective, the signifier "Rambler" signified a class of people inferior to we Kuenstlers.

For that matter, my dad made it clear that anyone who drove a Cadillac was just trying to make an impression, but had no sense of modesty or value. As with the Rambler, Cadillacs were not for *our* kind of people.

Our people drove *Oldsmobiles*.

My father owned Oldsmobiles for twenty seven consecutive years, starting with his first 1956 red and white two-tone Rocket 88, and ending with his last ride, a metallic blue 1981 Oldsmobile 98.

We lived among many other tribes–the Fords, the Chevrolets, the Chryslers, the Cadillacs, the Pontiacs, the

Buicks, and, yes, even the Ramblers. But we were the best. Only we Oldsmobiles understood the proper balance between value, performance, modern styling, and Protestant understatement.

I noted earlier that Roland Barthes said that automobiles had come to be perceived as magical. Surely my father sensed the magic inherent in his Oldsmobile.

Growing older, I came to understand much more about these brand tribes. In addition to the Oldsmobiles, there were tribes such as the Harley-Davidsons, the Calvin Kleins, the Martha Stewarts, the Targets, and the Apples.

Originally, I thought these brands were simply totems of membership.

Now, I know them as sometime articles of faith, bits of existential glue providing identity and meaning in a universe where mankind is unanchored from the ancient gods and their seminal myths.

One of Dad's existential anchors was his firm belief that an Oldsmobile would never let him down.

In the fifties and sixties, when each GM brand had its own strong identity, Olds was marketed to a psychographic group called the *executive innovator*. From the perspective of semiotics, the executive innovator's Oldsmobile signified to the world his character and integrity.

In a world where seemingly everything had been turned upside down from his birth in 1918 to his death, my father found few constants, and too many gremlins. That metallic blue 1981 Oldsmobile 98 four door with the eight-track tape player, sitting in in his driveway the night he died, was a vital part of his identity.

The very last of the Oldsmobiles, officially described as a cherry-red Alero sedan, rolled off the assembly line on April 29, 2004 in Lansing, Michigan, the same city where the brand was born. You can see it on display in Lansing's *R.E. Olds Transportation Museum*.

Oldsmobile, like my father, has joined the immortal Brand Gods.

About Walt Kuenstler

Walt has been in corporate and personal branding for more than forty years, having worked with clients such as The New York Times, Glaxo SmithKline, and Citic Securities International Partners.

His advertising career began in 1967 serving as an office boy with the Seiber & McIntyre advertising agency in Chicago. Graduating from the University of Pennsylvania with a BA in History, Walt found his way to McCann-Erickson in Manhattan, working in both Media and Account Service. He has held marketing positions with The New York Times, Ziff-Davis, and Playboy Magazine.

Today, he is President of Zolexa LTD, where he helps time-starved executives master new skills and stay ahead of the curve in current events and cultural trends impacting their businesses. China has become a particular interest of his. He has worked with Asia Society Los Angeles, The China-US Center for Sustainable Development, and the Shanghai company Xiao Nan Guo.

He specializes in designing marketing, branding, and public relations programs that leverage an individual's unique strengths, and delivering them through innovative media strategies. A pioneer in "book-driven branding", Walt was a founder of Winans Kuenstler Publishing, a personal branding initiative.

Walt graduated from the University of Pennsylvania with a BA in History. He lives outside of Philadelphia, Pennsylvania.

He can be reached though www.ZolexaLTD.com, and is on LinkedIn at http://www.linkedin.com/in/waltkuenstler.

Also by Walt Kuenstler

From The Sock Drawer:
Poems From 1970 And Beyond

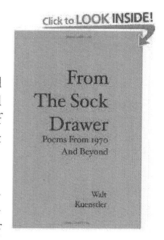

Click to **LOOK INSIDE!**

From
The Sock
Drawer
Poems From 1970
And Beyond

Walt
Kuenstler

Walt Kuenstler has offered up a selection of highly personal poetry in two segments: that of the voice of youth, and then that of maturity.

The first half of the book, written during his college years, strongly evokes life in the 1960s, the era of upheaval in politics, culture and the restructured idea of self-identity. Seen through the prismatic of university experience, young love and warnings of early addictive behavior, the poems show youth and innocence posturing bravely while looking into an uncertain future.

The second half of the book offers the voice of that same man, now mature and seasoned, a parent and householder. In a series of poems offering close attention to life's small cataclysms, Kuenstler illustrates the changes that occur within the scope of our lifetime. From youth's wrestle with the large issues to maturity's embrace of the microcosm as the hyper-real, we are offered to share the images and imaginings of one man's life in a way that is reflective of the lives we all lead.

Review by Debra Leigh Scott, founding director of Hidden River Arts.
Available from Amazon.com and other retailers
ISBN: 978-1439212073

INDEX

Made in the USA
Lexington, KY
03 November 2013